CON GAMES AND BROKEN HEARTS

INMATE ROMANCE SCAMS
EXPLAINED

AUTHOR:
LARRY JAY LEVINE

CO-AUTHOR:
KEISHA DAVIS

Con Games and Broken Hearts

Inmate Romance Scams Exposed
Copyright © 2025 Larry Jay Levine, Kiesha Davis
All rights reserved.

This book is a work of nonfiction based on the author's opinions, research, and personal experiences. The content herein is intended for informational purposes only and should not be construed as legal advice. While the author and publisher have made every effort to ensure the accuracy and completeness of the information presented, they make no guarantees and disclaim all liability for any errors, omissions, or outcomes resulting from the use of this book.

Legal Disclaimer:
The author and publisher are not lawyers. The strategies, insights, and opinions presented in this book are for informational purposes only and are not a substitute for professional legal advice. Readers are strongly advised to consult a licensed attorney for any legal concerns or questions related to their specific circumstances. By using the information in this book, you agree that the author and publisher will not be held liable for any outcomes resulting from its application.

First Edition
Printed in the United States of America

Publisher Information:
World Crime Media
New York, NY
For inquiries contact worldcrimemedia@gmail.com

213.948.1069

ISBN: 979-8-9921484-8-0

Additional Notes:
All names, dates, and specific details in any examples or case studies presented have been altered to protect the identities of those involved. Any resemblance to actual persons, living or dead, is purely coincidental unless otherwise stated.

Terms of Use:

TABLE OF CONTENTS

Introduction:
Wake Up Before You're Wiped Out

You ever look in the mirror and feel like you're holdin' it all down—loyal, ride-or-die, sacrificing like a damn soldier—and still somethin' feel *off*? Like you're pourin' everything you got into somebody who's locked up but somehow still got control over *you*?

Yeah. I've been there too.

This book ain't a love story. This ain't about prison reform. This is a goddamn *warning label* with lipstick stains and overdraft fees all over it.

This is for every woman who's been emotionally pimped out through a phone call, a promise, or a picture-perfect future that never existed outside his cellblock imagination.

I ain't here to judge you, baby. I'm here to save what's left of your dignity before he cashes in on that too.

You need to hear this before you're sittin' there wonderin' how the hell your whole life got hijacked by a motherfucker who can't even pee without permission.

Why This Book Exists

Because nobody told *me*.

Because when I was neck-deep in the lies, the manipulation, the mind games dressed up as love—I didn't have a manual. I had empty accounts, sleepless nights, and a man behind bars who played my emotions like a damn fiddle.

This book exists so **you** don't end up like that. So maybe *you* don't fall for the same recycled script that's been run on a thousand women before you. So *you* can finally see through the smoke before he sets your whole damn life on fire.

He don't love you like you love him. He loves **what you do for him**. He loves the *idea* of you—until commissary's loaded, your patience is drained, and he's on to the next chick with softer boundaries and a better job.

And the worst part? He *trained* you to accept that. Slowly. Sweetly. Strategically.

So now it's time for me to retrain you—to *unfuck your mind* before your heart costs you everything.

Who This Is For

This book is for the wives puttin' "Mrs. So-and-So" in their IG bios while their man's gettin' head from the block's biggest opportunist. It's for the girlfriends who done mastered Western Union and forgot what their own needs look like.

It's for the pen pals who think a dozen "good morning beautiful" texts mean more than a well-rehearsed hustle.

You still think you're *different*? That you're the *exception*? Girl, he told the same story to the last chick, the one before her, and five more lined up behind you.

If you're sending pictures, writing letters, moving money, or defending him to everyone who's raising red flags—this book is your *last call*. I ain't here to coddle you. I'm here to *crack the glass*. Because somebody has to. And I'm not scared to be the villain if it means you finally see the truth.

So turn the page, mama. It's time to stop being the victim of a jailhouse romance scam and start being the badass bitch you were before he got in your head.

Dedication

This book is for the women who gave until it hurt. The ones who stayed up late at night waiting on a phone call that never came, who held letters close like they were promises carved in stone, who emptied their wallets and poured out their hearts because they believed love could survive concrete and steel.

It's for the women who still carry the sting of betrayal — the shock of finding out that the sweet words weren't just for them, that the promises were cut-and-paste, and that the man they thought was their partner was really just playing another round of the same tired hustle. You didn't deserve that. You were never foolish for loving. You were human. And your humanity is not a weakness.

It's for the ones still in it right now — the women who can't bring themselves to admit what their gut already knows. You're clinging to hope, replaying excuses, covering lies with more lies. I see you. I've been you. And I wrote these pages so you don't have to stay stuck where I once was.

It's for the mothers, sisters, daughters, and best friends who watched from the outside — who saw the red flags and couldn't find the words to break through. This book is your voice now. It says what you've wanted to scream: *Wake up. Protect yourself. Your love should never be someone else's meal ticket.*

And yes, it's for the rare few men inside who are actually doing their time with honesty — no games, no scams, no scripts. You prove that not every inmate is a hustler. You remind us that integrity can exist even in a broken system. But you're the exception, not the rule. And this book needed to call out the rule.

Most of all, this book is for every woman who ever thought she was alone in this. You're not. You're standing in a long line of survivors — some scarred, some still bleeding, all stronger than they realize. This book is your mirror, your warning label, and your shield.

We put these words down so you never again confuse manipulation for devotion. So you never again trade your peace for someone else's hustle. So you never again hand your heart to a man who only sees it as another commissary account.

To the ones who've already walked away, to the ones still trapped, to the ones still deciding if that voice on the phone is worth the cost — this book belongs to you. Carry it, share it, and never forget: your love is worth more than somebody else's game.

— **Keisha & Larry**

Keisha Davis BIO & Dedication

I'm Keisha Davis, and let me tell you—nothing in this book comes from theory. I lived it. I got burned, I got played, and I paid the price. I grew up in Atlanta, raised by a single mom who busted her ass just to keep food on the table. That meant I learned early how to be sharp, street-smart, and ready for bullshit when it came knocking.

I hustled my way through school, worked two jobs to get my degree in paralegal studies, and thought I was building a safe career. But the truth is, I never had patience for filing paperwork and sitting quietly in courtrooms. My thing was always sniffing out lies and exposing the game for what it really is. And life made sure I got a front-row seat to the dirtiest game of all: prison romance hustles.

At twenty-eight, I fell for Devon, a man doing time who knew exactly how to write the perfect letter. Sweet words, promises of forever, dreams of "when I get out." For two years, I believed it. I sent him money, trusted him, and ignored every red flag. By the end, I was down twelve grand and realized I wasn't his "ride or die"—I was just another mark on his list. That betrayal nearly broke me, but instead, it built me.

I turned that pain into fuel. Today, I'm a private investigator who specializes in fraud and prison scams. I help women see the signs before they get too deep, and I don't sugarcoat a damn thing. I've been there. I know what it feels like to love someone behind bars and not realize you're being played until it's too late. That's why I do what I do—because no woman deserves to learn the hard way like I did.

I'm loyal, I'm blunt, and I don't hand out trust for free anymore. But when I see another woman walking the same path I once walked, I step in. Not as some polished expert, but as someone who's been in the trenches and found her way out.

And this book? It's bigger than me. Jay and I came together to make sure the truth gets told. He's got the inside perspective from serving time, I've got the scars from being on the outside looking in—and together, we're blowing the lid off the con games too many women fall for. If you're reading this, understand one thing: I'm not here to lecture you. I'm here to hand you the map I wish someone gave me before I lost years of my life and money I'll never get back.

Dedication

To my mama—who worked herself half to death but still raised me to stand tall, even when the world tried to knock me down. You didn't have much to give, but what you gave was grit, and that carried me further than money ever could.

To Marlene—my mentor, my rock, the one who showed me how to take pain and flip it into power. Without your guidance, I'd still be stuck in the wreckage. You handed me the tools to rebuild, and I'll never forget that.

To every woman I've sat with, cried with, and fought for—this book carries your stories too. You made me realize I wasn't alone, and that's why I'll never stop fighting for you.

And finally, to Larry Levine—when I picked up Prison Politics 101, I didn't just read another book. I found a voice that spoke the raw truth about the system, and that's how our paths crossed. From that connection, this book was born.

—Keisha

Larry Levine BIO & Dedication

Larry Levine didn't study the prison hustle from behind a desk—he lived it. After doing ten years in eleven different federal prisons for conspiracy, securities fraud, racketeering, and obstruction of justice, he walked out with a mission: to expose the system and the dirty games it breeds.

He's the author of multiple no-bullshit books that pull the curtain back on the so-called justice system: *Crimes That Never Happened*, *Prison Politics 101*, *Lies My Lawyer Told Me*, and *The Art of Dealing with Two-Faced People*. His writing isn't sanitized, politically correct, or softened for mainstream comfort—and that's exactly why people listen.

Major media outlets have been calling on Larry for over a decade. He's appeared on CNN, Fox News, MSNBC, Court TV, HLN, CBS, ABC Nightline, Newsmax, Inside Edition, and more—breaking down high-profile cases and prison dynamics with brutal honesty and insider insight. He's worked with Anderson Cooper, Ashleigh Banfield, Neil Cavuto, Shep Smith, Dr. Drew, and others who know when the truth matters, Larry delivers.

But behind the books and the media hits, Larry's a husband, a father, and a grandfather—loyal to the people who stood by him when the system tried to erase him. That loyalty is what brought him into this project. After connecting with Keisha Davis through his book *Prison Politics 101*, they teamed up to make *Con Games* the street-smart guide every woman in a prison relationship needs.

Larry Levine isn't here to make prison look good. He's here to blow the lid off the lies, torch the fairy tale, and make sure the next woman doesn't become just another name in another inmate's playbook.

Dedication

To the ones still locked behind bars—this is for you. The system chewed you up, stripped you of your name, stamped a number on your chest, and called it justice. But I see you. The fighters. The thinkers. The ones who got buried by broken laws, shady prosecutors, and court-appointed cowards who were more loyal to the calendar than your defense.

Some of you were guilty. Some of you were stupid. But a whole lot of you? You were set up. Overcharged. Lied on. Sold out. You caught more time than you should've because the Feds don't play fair and the court system sure as hell doesn't hand out second chances unless there's something in it for them.

To the wrongly convicted—the ones doing time for crimes you didn't commit— I don't have the words to undo the hell you're living. But I'm not gonna lie to you and tell you "justice will prevail." Because it didn't. It hasn't. And it won't— not unless we force it to. This book isn't about hope. It's about truth. Ugly, raw, system-exposing truth.

You're the reason I write. You're the reason I keep lighting fires under this fake-ass system's feet. You're the reason I stopped playing nice a long time ago. Because someone has to say what the lawyers won't. Someone has to call bullshit on the judges, the prosecutors, the agents, and the snakes in suits who profit off destruction.

So here it is. No apologies. No sugarcoating. Just the truth, loud and pissed off.

And to the men I did time with—the real ones, not the ones who folded when it got hard—you taught me how to survive. You showed me how deep the rabbit hole goes. You reminded me that even in a place built to break people, some of us stay unbreakable.

This one's for you. For all of you.

—Larry Levine

Published Works

Prison Politics 101
An insider's survival guide to the unwritten rules, power plays, and politics that run every prison yard.

Crimes That Never Happened: Beating Federal Conspiracies
Exposes how the feds stack fake charges and teaches how to dismantle conspiracy cases before they bury you.

Lies My Lawyer Told Me – Prelude to Justice
A brutal breakdown of the lies, tricks, and betrayals that defendants face from their own lawyers before trial.

Cookinn in the Clink
Prison food, hustles, and survival recipes straight from the tiers — raw stories mixed with jailhouse ingenuity.

The Art of Dealing with Two-Faced People
A no-bullshit manual for spotting liars, manipulators, and snakes before they get the chance to burn you.

Coming Soon

The Courtroom Conspiracy
 Pulls the mask off prosecutors, judges, and courtroom insiders who twist the system for their own gain. A raw, unapologetic look at how justice really works once you step inside the courtroom.

Rules of Engagement: Running a Dirty Political Campaign
 The gloves come off in this brutal playbook on how campaigns are really won — with manipulation, optics, and psychological warfare, not policy papers and handshakes.

The Art of Manipulating Your Significant Other
 A dark, unfiltered guide to control, power, and influence in relationships. It's not about romance — it's about leverage, dominance, and winning the emotional battlefield.

Mind Games: The Dark Art of Business Warfare
 Exposes the ruthless tactics behind boardroom success — psychological manipulation, silent sabotage, and the strategies that separate predators from prey in business.

Welcome to the Circus

What These Modules Cover

This is where the whole scam kicks off, sweetheart. Module 1 ain't romance, it's a fucking sideshow where the main act is you getting played. He reels you in with sob stories, dumps out trauma like it's half-off at a yard sale, sprinkles in some Hallmark "you're my queen" bullshit, and packages it all up like he's offering you forever. Reality check: he ain't building shit but a hustle — and **you're the building material**.

CHAPTER 1 – The Sob Story Formula

This is the sympathy hook. He weaponizes tears, childhood tragedies, and "the system did me dirty" monologues to make you think you're Florence Nightingale saving a lost soul. Newsflash: you're not a healer, you're a mark.

CHAPTER 2 – The Fantasy Package

Letters dipped in cheap perfume and fake promises. He paints castles in the sky — businesses, houses, kids, forever-and-ever crap — while you're footing the bill for ramen spreads and phone time.

CHAPTER 3 – The Love Bomb Cycle

Compliments on crack. He floods you with "baby you so fine" until you're addicted, then flips the script into guilt trips and jealousy games. It's not affection — it's psychological warfare with emojis.

CHAPTER 4 – Guardrails Ain't Weakness

This one's your lifeline. It's where we show you how to stop chasing, stop apologizing for shit you didn't do, and stop financing Captain Bullshit. Guardrails don't make you weak — they keep you from turning into an ATM with tits.

The Real Takeaway

Module 1 is about ripping the glitter off the con so you can see it for what it is: a playbook that's been passed around the yard longer than a Hustler magazine. Every sob story, every sweet letter, every fake "forever" — it's all designed to gut your wallet and chain your emotions. You're not his queen, you're not his miracle, and you're damn sure not his future. You're his payday.

And if you don't learn these tricks early? You're gonna pay for his smokes, his snacks, and his side-pieces — while patting yourself on the back for being "the only one who understands him." That's not love. That's you being the punchline to the same tired joke.

CHAPTER ONE

The Sob Story Formula

§1.1 The Oldest Hustle in the Yard

Alright girl, listen up. I'm Keisha, and this shit you walking into, hooking up with a man inside, I been there myself. Devon had me wrapped up like a Christmas present, bow and all. Thought he was my "one and only," when in reality, he was running the same tired play that damn near every inmate knows by heart: the **sob story**. This is the first fucking trick in their book, and they polish it like their little jailhouse trophy.

These dudes been practicing that act since the minute they hit the joint. They know the lines, the tears, the sighs — like they auditioning for a prison soap opera. And you? You get cast as the savior. It's their signature move, and if you ain't hip to it, you'll dive in headfirst.

The Script Every Fool Rehearses

Here's how it always kicks off: "I wasn't always like this. I was good, but life did me dirty." Girl, please. That's the hook — bait on the fishing line. They not serving you truth; they spoon-feeding you pity because pity the fastest way into a woman's heart.

Then comes the backstory you've heard a hundred times before. Bad childhood, mama on drugs, daddy gone, the streets raised him, made some dumb choices, ended up behind bars, *but now he's different*. Sound familiar? That's cause it's tired-ass, passed-around bullshit. They don't even change the ingredients — it's the same damn recipe passed down cell to cell like ramen spreads.

Pity as a Weapon

The hustle work because women like us got compassion. We see pain, we wanna heal it. That the setup. He makes you feel like you the only one who "really gets him," the only one who sees past the bars into the heart of a misunderstood man. And that when you slide from lover into savior.

You start thinking: *Maybe I can help him. Maybe I'm the one who can turn his life around.* Newsflash: you not his salvation. You his **target**. He aint looking for a damn fix to his life — he looking for someone to carry the load, and he already picked y our ass to play that role.

The Theater of Tears

Don't think for a second this spontaneous. It's soap opera bullshit. Every crack in the voice, every watery eye, every deep sigh — it's rehearsed. They run this act so many times they could win an Emmy. And while you wiping his imaginary tears, he's clocking how much of your energy, your time, and your heart he can drain the hell outta you before you catch on.

Picture it: you pouring yourself out, believing every tragic beat of his "life story," while he kicked back in his cell, running the same lines on three other women. That ain't vulnerability. That's a fuckin audition and you not the co-star in his redemption arc; you just another sucker in the bleachers.

How I Fell for It

Let me be real with you. Devon sold me the exact same script. "Keisha, life wasn't fair to me. My mama was gone, my daddy locked up, and I had no one." Motherfucker sounded so damn sincere, like I was his last hope. And what did I do? I swallowed it whole, thinking I be the one to give him love he never had. That the danger of the sob story — it hijacks your compassion. You stop listening to your gut, you start living in *his* pain instead of watching his actions. I was so wrapped up in being the "only one who understood him" that I didn't even notice I was being played.

The Part That Fucked Me Up

That's the cold truth of this formula: the sob story is just the bait. The real trap is what comes after. Once you believe his "innocent man done wrong" act, he's got ammo to guilt trip your ass. You feel guilty saying no, because now you the one "abandoning him" just like everybody else. He don't even have to beg loud — just a sad look, a sigh, a "baby, you don't know how much you mean to me." Suddenly, you reaching for your wallet, your phone, your time, your energy.

Killing the Fairytale

Here what you need to tattoo on your brain: **that sob story ain't truth — it's theater.** And you? You not the chosen one, you not his miracle, and you damn sure not the savior he's pretending to need. You just the next mark in line.

The only way to win is to stop buying tickets to the same play. The lines don't change, the cast don't change, the ending sure as hell don't change. You walk in thinking you gonna save him, but really you just paying to watch yourself get hustled.

So now that you've read this far, pay attention. I'm gonna show you how to dodge the trap, protect your wallet, and save yourself a world of hurt — because once you see through the sob story, you can't unsee it. And that's when you take your power back.

§1.2 The Sweet Talk Trap

When Love Bombs Feel Like Roses

That how it starts: he hits you with a flood of sweetness so thick you forget to breathe. "You so fine." "I never met nobody like you." "You the one I been waiting for." Every word drips like honey, and you sitting there glowing like a damn light bulb, thinking you finally found someone who sees you. Feels good, right? That's the setup. But don't get it twisted — that ain't love. That's strategy.

See, compliments are the cheapest hustle in the book. Doesn't cost them shit, but it pays out heavy. The more he praises you, the more you feel special, chosen, different from every other chick he ever dealt with. But truth is, you ain't different. You just the next. And the second you start believing his sweet talk, you walked right into the trap.

Sweet Words, Heavy Chains

Let me tell you how this really works. When a man praises you nonstop like you Jesus in heels, he ain't worshipping you — he's working you. Every "you so fine" is a rope tying you closer. Every "you the one" is another knot. Before long, you wrapped up so tight in that asshole you don't even see how little you actually know about him.

And the wild part? He ain't even creative. It's the same Hallmark one-line hand me down bull shit over and over. Don't believe me? Ask three different women who wrote to the same dude in county jail — they'll all swear they heard the exact same lines. Because they did.

The Glow That Blinds You

Here's why it works: people crave validation. A dude who hypes you up every day makes you feel like you finally found what's been missing. You're walking on clouds, smiling at texts like a teenager, forgetting all about reality. That's what makes it dangerous.

I was there myself. Devon had me blushing through phone calls, grinning like a damn fool. Every time he said, "Keisha, you the most beautiful woman I ever met," I let it slide even though I knew deep down it sounded rehearsed. Why? Because I wanted that shit to be real so bad, I damn near lost my mind. That's the trap — wanting the words so bad you ignore the fact they're empty.

Closing the Trap

Sweet talk ain't the endgame. It is the door opener. Once he's got you cheesin' off compliments, he shifts gears. Suddenly he's "opening up" — sliding into vulnerability mode. "I been hurt before." "Nobody ever held me down like you do." He paints himself as a broken man who just needs the right woman. Guess who's cast for that role? You.

By now, the sweet talk already hooked your heart. Now the "broken man" act hooks your loyalty. He's stacking layers — first make you feel worshipped, then make you feel needed. And once you feel needed, you'll start doing anything to prove you deserve that pedestal he put you on.

The Hallmark Playbook

Let's break down some of the classic lines:

"I never met nobody like you." → Translation: *you number 87, but I'll make you feel like number one.*

"You the one I been waiting for." → Translation: *This is exactly what I told the last girl, but hey, it worked on her too.*

"I can't stop thinking about you." → Translation: *I've got 23 hours a day in this cell, of course I can't stop thinking — I don't got cable.*

And the kicker? They'll write these same lines in letters to two, three, sometimes four women at once. It's like a copy-paste scam — except the women on the other end think they're reading poetry straight from the soul.

When Sweet Turns Sour

Here's the part most women miss: the compliments don't stay free. They always come with strings. "You so fine" soon turns into "You deserve better than this — if only I had a little help, I could give you the world." See it? He lays the foundation with flattery, then builds the ask on top of it.

I've seen women drain bank accounts because they were so hooked on hearing "baby, you my queen." They believed the fantasy so deep, they didn't realize those words were just hot air blown straight up your ass to keep you blind while your money vanished

Keisha's Reality Check

Listen — ain't nothing wrong with a man complimenting you. Real men do it, too. But here's the test: compliments without real shit to back it up just con games. If the sweet talk comes heavy and fast but the actions don't match? That's not love. That straight up hustle..

You gotta stop asking, "Does he make me feel good?" and start asking, "Do his actions line up with his words?" Because if the only proof of his love is a handful of tired-ass one-liners, you not in love — you in a hustle.

Closing the Trap Door

The Sweet Talk Trap ain't about romance, it's about control. Words are weapons in the hands of a hustler, and if you don't recognize the game, you'll get cut deep. So here's the takeaway: pay attention not to the compliments, but to the consistency. If the words ain't backed by effort, time, and proof? Stop listening.

A man who truly sees you don't repeat Hallmark clichés like a broken record. He'll show you. Anything less? That's just a con dressed in pretty words. And if you learn to spot it early, you'll save yourself months, maybe years, of heartbreak and wasted money.

§1.3 The Vulnerability Trap

The Script Flip

Once he's buttered you up with sweet talk and had you cheesin' like a kid at prom, he flips the damn script. Now it ain't about how fine you are or how you "the one." Nope. Now it's about him being broken. You'll hear lines like, "I been hurt before," or "Nobody ever held me down like you do." And just like that, you not the goddess anymore — you the therapist, the savior, the one who's supposed to fix what every other woman "destroyed."

This is strategic as hell. Because once you step into the role of "healer," you not just loving him anymore — you working for him.

The Power of a Sad Story

Let's break it down. Vulnerability, when it's real, can build intimacy. But in the wrong hands, it's just another hustle. These dudes know women love feeling needed. It taps straight into your instinct to nurture, to protect, to love harder when someone looks fragile. And they flip that shit into a hustle.

He'll confess about his ex who cheated. Or he'll talk about being abandoned by family. He might even fake tears on the phone. Every "I never had nobody like you" is designed to push you deeper into his pocket. Because now, if you walk away, you just another person who "let him down."

My Own Lesson

Devon ran this play on me too. After weeks of sweet talk, he hit me with the "I don't know what I'd do without you" routine. I thought I was special, like I was healing some deep wound nobody else could touch. He told me about his childhood, about how he was always overlooked, about how I was the first person who truly saw him.

You know what I did? I doubled down. I started sending more letters, more commissary money, even calling his mama to make sure she was okay. I thought I was proving my love. In reality, I was just volunteering as his unpaid emotional support hotline.

The Savior Setup

Here's the catch — when you start feeling like you the only one keeping him alive, you've already lost. That's the **savior setup**. You start carrying his baggage like it's yours, patching up wounds you didn't create. Meanwhile, he's sitting back, smiling, because now he's got you locked.

Think about it: if he's always broken, you always busy fixing. And when you busy fixing him, you ain't noticing that he's playing you.

The Illusion of Change

This hustle is slick because it dangles hope. He'll say things like, "With you, I can finally be a better man." And for a minute, you believe it. You think you building him into something real, that your love is the missing piece. But here's the ugly truth: he don't want to change. Change means accountability, effort, and growth — none of which fit into a hustler's agenda.

He wants the benefits of you thinking he's changing without doing a damn thing different. And as long as you believe in his "brokenness," he can stay lazy, irresponsible, and manipulative — all while you pick up the slack.

Signs you Being Played

How do you spot the Vulnerability Trap? Look for patterns:

He "opens up" quick, but it's the same lines recycled every time.

His pain always centers him — never about you, never mutual.

Every story has the same ending: he's the victim, and you the only one who can fix it.

When you try to pull back, he guilt-trips you with "Don't leave me, I can't survive without you."

Those ain't confessions — they're chains.

Keisha's Reality Check

Let me hit you with the truth: his brokenness ain't yours to fix. And if he's leaning on you to be his savior, that's not vulnerability — that manipulation. Real vulnerability comes with growth. It says, "Here's my pain, and here's how I'm working on it." Fake vulnerability just dumps the weight on your ass and calls it love.

I wasted months being Devon's emotional crutch. While I was crying with his sorry ass, hoping my love would patch his wounds, he was running the same routine on other women, painting himself as "misunderstood." That's the part that burned the most — realizing I wasn't special, I was just the next nurse in line.

Closing the Wound

If you take one thing from this, let it be this: vulnerability without action is a hustle. Don't let him sell you his brokenness like it's a diamond in the rough. It ain't. It's just another trick to keep you hooked, loyal, and blind.

You don't need to fix a man to be loved. You don't need to heal someone else's wounds to prove your worth. If he's truly broken, that's his work to do — not yours. And if he's weaponizing his pain to keep you in place? That ain't love, sis. That's prison-grade manipulation.

§1.4 The Illusion of Love: Selling You a Dream

The Future He Can't Deliver

By now, you already knee-deep in the game. First, he fed you the sob story, then he buttered you up with compliments, then he played the broken man. Now he's ready to lock you down for good. This is where he pulls out the big guns: the dream. He paints it so pretty you can almost see it. Marriage, kids, a house together, businesses, vacations, a whole life that sounds too good to pass up. And while you sitting there picturing forever, he's sitting there scheming his next hustle.

The smoke and mirrors bullshit of love the sharpest blade in the hustler's playbook. It's designed to cut you off from reality and keep you believing in something that never existed in the first place.

How They Sell the Dream

It always starts with whispers of the future. "When I get out, we're gonna build something together." "We'll start a family, buy a house, live the life I never had." Those words hit deep, because they speak to your own hopes. He's not inventing new dreams —he just repackagin' your shit and sellin' it back to you like a damn used car salesman

The more details he adds, the harder is for you to pull away. He'll describe the house. He'll talk about what the kids' names will be. He'll swear up and down that he's never felt like this before, that you the reason he's finally ready to be a better man. It's smoke and mirrors girl, he's building castles out of your own imagination while he sits behind concrete walls.

Why We Fall for It

Let's keep it real — women fall for the Illusion of Love because hope is powerful. After dealing with disappointment, heartbreak, and half-assed men, the idea of someone dreaming with you feels like oxygen. You want to believe he's different. You want to believe this time, it's real.

I was guilty of it too. Devon had me planning businesses we'd never start, talking about houses we'd never buy, living out fantasies in my head that never left the prison yard. I thought I was building with him when really, I was building for him.

The Red Flags You Ignore

The scariest part of this hustle is how it blinds you to reality. You stop noticing the red flags because you too busy chasing the dream. You overlook the inconsistencies, the empty promises, the way he always has an excuse for why he can't show proof. You ignore your gut because your heart high on a fairy tale ending that aint never coming!

And that's the goal: keep you distracted with a fantasy long enough that by the time the mask slips, you've already invested everything. Your best years, your best energy, sometimes your whole damn bank account — gone in service of a love that never existed.

The Trap Inside the Promise

Understand this: the dream is not a gift, it's a cage. Once you believe in it, you chain yourself to it. You keep sacrificing because "one day it'll all be worth it." But that "one day" never comes. He's not thinking about the family, the house, or the business. He's thinking about how to keep you locked in long enough to get what he needs now.

The Illusion of Love is nothing more than a leash, and the tighter you hold onto it, the easier it is for him to pull you wherever he wants you to go.

Keisha's Reality Check

Here's the cold truth: real love ain't a story he feeds you from a cell. Real love is consistency, effort, action. If all he's offering are words about a future you can't touch, then you not in love — you in a play he scripted to keep you around.

I lived it. I chased a dream that was nothing but smoke, and when the smoke cleared, I was left standing alone, broke, drained and played. Don't let that be you. Don't let him sell you on a forever that evaporates the second he done using you.

Take Your Power Back

The Illusion of Love only works if you keep buying into it. The second you stop believing his words and start demanding proof, the fantasy collapses. And when it collapses, you finally see him for what he is — not a man building a future, but a hustler protecting his present.

You don't owe anybody your years, your money, or your loyalty just because they dangle a picture of forever in front of your face. Real love grows slow, proves itself, and shows up every damn day. Don't get caught chasing castles in the air while he's probably laughin' his damn ass off, countin' commissary dollars you sent him.

The only way to win is to recognize the dream for what it is: an illusion. And the second you see it clear, you take your power back.

§1.5 Raven Sinclair Commentary

I've been there — staring at letters like they were gospel, rereading them late at night because I wanted so damn badly to believe a man behind bars could mean every word he wrote. I told myself, "He sounds sincere. He must be different." Meanwhile, he was mailing the same shit to three other women, just swapping out the names. I didn't know it then, but I was one of many. That realization didn't just sting — it gutted me.

I remember the first time I sent money. It was "just $40" for commissary. No big deal, right? Then it was another $60. Then another "favor." By the time I woke up, I had drained hundreds — not just from my account, but from my peace of mind. I was losing sleep, making excuses, hiding it from my friends because deep down I knew I was being played. But I still wanted to believe I was the one.

Here's the truth I had to choke down: wanting to believe doesn't make it real. And every time I doubled down, I was digging my own hole deeper. That's the ugliest part of the sob story scam — you don't just lose money. You lose yourself. You stop trusting your gut. You ignore the red flags. You confuse pity with love.

But I clawed my way out. I stopped answering letters. I stopped sending money. And the minute I cut him off, the silence told me everything I needed to know. No fight for me, no desperate call, no "please don't leave." Just nothing. Because it was never about me — it was about what I could provide.

So hear me clearly: if you're living in this chapter right now, don't wait for a bigger betrayal to wake you up. Stop romanticizing struggle. Stop thinking your love will rewrite his story. You're not his cure. You're his supply. And the second you cut that off, you get to start writing your own damn story again. One where you're not drained, not lied to, and not used. One where you're free.

§1.6 Larry Levine Commentary

I did 10 in the Feds and seen this shit live from the inside, so let me save you some fucking suspense and clue you in: 1) you weren't his savior, 2) you weren't his queen, and 3) you sure as fuck weren't "the only one who ever understood him." You were his bitch and a walking fucking ATM with a pulse. That's it. And the part that stings? You signed up for it. You volunteered to play Florence Nightingale to a con man who's been crying on cue since he figured out women love a "hurt little boy" story.

Here's the fucking truth you don't wanna swallow: that sad-ass shit about his mama, his daddy, his hard-knock life? He's been running that scam longer than you've been paying bills. It's rehearsed. It's fake. And you bought it like front row tickets to a show called *"Sucker: The Musical."*

And while you were busy reading his letters and fingering yourself, sending him money and wiping imaginary tears, and patting yourself on the back for being "the one who gets him," guess what? He was running the same tired lines on two other women trying to score some pussy at the same damn time. You weren't chosen. You were disposable and rotated.

So here's your wake-up call ladies: the next time some asshole locked up starts spilling trauma like he's auditioning for *America's Saddest Inmate*, don't reach for your wallet — reach for the fucking door. Because you can either be the mark or you can be the one who finally says no. And if you still fall for it after reading this? Then congratulations, sweetheart. You don't just deserve to get hustled — you're begging for it. You got free money you wanna give away, send it to me and I can feed you the same fucking lines. Now pay attention to what we gotta say in the book because we are gonna save your ass a world of fucking hurt!!

CHAPTER TWO

The Fantasy Package

§2.1 Predator Mindset – You Ain't in Love, You the Prey

You Ain't in Love, You Lunch

Let's kill the fairytale quick—you ain't in love. You the prey. That man don't see you as his queen, his blessing, his forever. Nah, baby, you a target. He don't care about your heart, he care about what come with it—your money, your loyalty, your time, your energy. Hell, if you let him, he'll drain your soul and smile while doin' it.

You think he looking for a partner? Girl, please. He looking for someone to be his bitch, someone he can control. He moving with that predator mindset, and predators don't play fair—they hunt. Sweet talk, fake vulnerability, sad-ass stories—all of it just bait. He don't need you, he need what you can provide. You ain't his love, you his lick.

Sizing You Up

The first thing a hustler like this gonna' do is study you. Not in no romantic way—nah, he scannin' like a damn blueprint. He watchin' what makes you tick, what makes you weak, what you thirsty for. You lonely? He gonna' sell you "forever." You a fixer? He gonna show up "broken." You been hurt before? He gonna play the one man who "understands."

And peep this—he'll listen to you talk for hours, nod like he care, but notice how he never say much about himself? That ain't intimacy, sis, that's recon. He takin' notes, sizing up just how much he can get, how far he can push. Once he clock your soft spot? Boom. Switch flipped.

Now you the one carryin' the load, responsible for his happiness, his survival, his whole damn vibe.

Guilt: The Favorite Weapon

Once you hooked, here come the guilt trips. Classic. *"You the only one who been here for me." "I don't know what I'd do without you." "Everybody else left me but you."* Man, get the fuck outta here.

But it works, don't it? It hit your heart. You feel needed. You feel like the savior. You start thinkin', *"If I just hang on, maybe I can help him change."* But lemme tell you: he ain't changin'. He don't want to. That's the trap. The guilt ain't about gratitude—it's about control. He know if you feel responsible for his emotions, you'll keep sacrificin' yours.

It Ain't Love, It's Game

This where you gotta wake up. What you feelin' ain't love, it's manipulation gift-wrapped pretty. He studyin' you, usin' your kindness like currency, runnin' plays that been perfected over years. And you? You fallin' in love with a performance.

Predators don't fix themselves. They don't need fixin'. They need feedin'. And the minute you stop feedin' 'em what they want? They fucking gone. Next chick, same lines. It's a cycle, and unless you see it for what it is, you just the next one in rotation.

Recognize It Before It's Too Late

So here's your escape route: the moment he make you feel guilty for sayin' no—run. The moment he try to make you responsible for his happiness—run. The moment he crown you "the only one who understands" two weeks in—run faster.

You ain't the first woman he told this to, and you won't be the last if you stick around. But you don't gotta be another victim. Spot the predator mindset early, before you deep in. Protect your peace, your bag, your heart. 'Cause if you don't, he gonna take it all—and leave you wonderin' how you let it happen.

§2.2 Emotional Profiling – Finding Your Weak Spots

Sizing You Up: How They Spot the Cracks

First thing these dudes gonna do? They watchin'. Not 'cause they in love, not 'cause they care—nah, they runnin' recon. Every word out your mouth, every little story you tell, they clockin' it. You mention how your last man cheated? Boom—that's a note. You say you always felt overlooked? Boom—that's another. You think he's just listenin' sweet? Hell no, that motherfucker is clockin' every word. He's buildin' his playbook off your pain.

And it ain't random. They sit there quiet, noddin', lettin' you talk while they takin' mental notes: what makes you light up, what makes you cry, what keeps you up at night. Then later? They feed it back to you like they "get" you. *"Baby, I would never hurt you like that."* *"You deserve somebody who sees you."* Sound familiar? Yeah, it's not him bein' real—it's him usin' your own words to trap you.

The "I Need You" Routine

Once he know your weak spots, here comes the big con: *"I need you."* Girl, the fuck he do. He ain't need you, he need what you bringin'. That line right there is the emotional hook. You hear it and start feelin' chosen, like maybe you the one who can fix him, the one who can turn him around. Nah. That ain't need— that's manipulation.

Watch how it play: he'll hit you with stories 'bout how hard life's been, how nobody stuck around, how broken he is. Then he slide in, *"But you, baby—you the only one holdin' me down."* And now you out here feelin' like Wonder Woman with a cape on your back. But the truth? You just fell right into the script. He don't want saving. He want supply.

The Guilt Game: Flippin' the Script

Soon as you start pullin' back or questionin' shit, he gonna flip it. Quick. *"Damn, you switchin' up on me."* *"I thought you was different, now you lettin' me down."* See that? Now you the villain. He set you up from day one, made you feel responsible for his whole emotional state, so now any time you say no, it feels like you breakin' him.

That's the game—he make you question yourself. You go from *"he needs me"* to *"maybe I ain't doin' enough."* And the second you start doubtin' yourself, he got you locked. You stop focusin' on your own needs, your own worth, 'cause you too busy carryin' his fuckin' emotional baggage like it's yours.

Trust Your Gut: The Red Flags Don't Lie

Here's the thing: your gut know. It always know. When somethin' feel off? It is. You ever notice how fast he talk about trust, loyalty, love—but don't really show none of it? That's the mask slippin'. Don't ignore that uneasy feelin' just 'cause he talkin' pretty. That flattery, that deep "understanding," it ain't genuine—it's profiling. He's studyin' you like a test he already know the answers to.

Break the Fucking Cycle

So how you beat it? Stop lettin' him probe. Stop givin' him your playbook. You don't owe him your insecurities, your past trauma, your damn life story in week two. Guard that shit. The minute you hear that "I need you" line, that guilt trip, that over-the-top flattery—you already know the play. That ain't love, that's a setup.

And the best move? Run. Not explain, not argue, not try to "prove" yourself. Run. The second you stop feedin' the game, you take back control. He'll move on to the next chick, 'cause that's what predators do. But you? You'll walk away with your power intact, and that's the win.

§2.3 The "We'll Make It Together" Trap

The Dream They Sell You

Girl, lemme holler at you about that tired-ass *"when I get out, we'll build a life together"* line. You know the one—*"We'll get a house, I'll work a good job, we'll be solid."* Yeah, sounds sweet. Sounds like stability. But baby, it's straight fiction. He feedin' you that Disney Channel script to keep you locked in. While you daydreamin' about love and a white picket fence, he sittin' there plottin' on how to make his future happen—by ridin' on your back.

And don't get it twisted—his "future" and your future ain't the same. Yours got sacrifice, love, work, maybe even kids and real bills. His? That man just tryna make sure he got somebody to cosign his bullshit while he slides right back into the same hustle that landed him in a cell.

The Load-Bearing Woman

Let's be real—*building together* always end up bein' code for *you buildin' while he chillin'*. You workin' two jobs, holdin' down the bills, runnin' to see him on visits, sendin' money, listenin' to his problems. And him? He sittin' back writin' love letters like that bullshit means something!

He don't wanna share the load—he want you to carry it. Every dollar you send, every tear you shed, every promise you keep—that's the bricks in this "future" y'all buildin'. Only problem? You the only one layin' bricks. He sittin' back watchin' the house go up, already schemin' about what room he gonna claim first.

The Real Hustle Behind the Fairytale

And sis, don't sleep on this part—the "we'll make it together" trap ain't just about money, it's emotional too. He keep you investin', over and over, 'cause he know once you deep in, you'll stick around. You'll think, *"Well, I already gave him three years, I can't just walk away."* That's the hook. He want you feelin' like you in too deep to back out.

But peep the hustle—while you sacrificin' everything for a future that don't exist, he steady practicin' manipulation. You the fucking rehearsal. By the time he out? He already trained on how to get the next chick to fund him quicker than you did.

Keisha's Reality Check

Look, real love don't need no *"one day"* fairy tale. Real love show up in the present. If he ain't showin' you consistency, respect, and effort while he locked up, what make you think it gonna magically appear when he touch free world? Girl, if he ain't doin' it now, he sure as hell ain't gonna do it later.

That "we'll make it together" line is just another way to keep you loyal, keep you broke, keep you emotionally exhausted. You out here bendin' over backwards while he just ridin' shotgun in a car you bought and gassed up and that sorry motherfucker ain't even sayin' thank you. That ain't partnership—that's slavery with lipstick on it.

Keisha's Closing Advice

Sis, stop chasin' that fantasy. If a man can't show you respect and real effort *today*, there ain't no tomorrow with him worth waitin' on. A man that got real love for you gonna put in work right now—even behind bars. He gonna speak to you with honesty, he gonna show appreciation, he gonna move different. If he just feedin' you promises about a future you can't see? That ain't love. That's game.

And lemme give it to you raw: the only thing you "makin' together" in that setup is excuses. Don't waste your years buildin' castles in the sky for a m

§2.4 The Long Game – Patience is Their Biggest Weapon

The Slow Hustle

Girl, here's what you gotta understand—these men ain't playin' short-term. They not rushin', they not desperate. They patient as hell, and that patience? That's their sharpest weapon. You out here wantin' results, wantin' love to move fast, thinkin' "if he says this now, maybe he mean it." But nah. He don't need quick. He got all the time in the world to stretch this out, keep you hangin', keep you dreamin'.

While you sittin' there waitin' on the payoff, he settin' the stage. He buildin' his hustle brick by brick, makin' sure by the time you wake up, you already too invested to walk.

How They Build You Up Piece by Piece

This ain't no love story, it's construction work. They layin' one emotional brick at a time—"you so beautiful," "nobody ever understood me like you," "one day we gonna build together." They sprinkle it slow, like breadcrumbs, and you keep followin'. And before you even notice? Boom—you knee deep emotionally, and you can't remember how you got there.

But don't mistake that patience for devotion. That's manipulation with a long fuse. They smart enough not to blow their cover early. They drip-feed you just enough "realness" to make you hold on, but never enough to actually give you what you want.

Push, Pull, Repeat

Patience equals control, baby. That's the whole formula. When you get too close, they pull back. When you start to pull back, they pop back in with some bullshit sweet talk. It's like push-pull, hot-cold, over and over. You always feel off-balance, and that's the point.

They keep you chasin'. And the longer you chasin', the harder it is to quit. You hooked on the highs and lows, like a damn slot machine in Vegas with no payout. One sweet text, one "I miss you," one "we gonna be good"—and you back in it, thinkin' this time it's different. Spoiler: it ain't.

Why You Stay So Long

See, the crazy part? You know the red flags are there. But you ignore 'em 'cause you invested. You already poured your time, your heart, your energy, maybe even your money. You think, *"I done gave too much to walk away now, I gotta see it through."* That's the fucking trap. They want you so tangled up that leavin' feels like losin'.

Truth is—you already losin'. Every day you stay, you losin' a little more of yourself. And he? He just playin' the same old tune, smilin' while you convince yourself to keep waitin'.

Keisha's Reality Check

Let me hit you with it raw: this ain't a man with patience. This a man with a hustle. He draggin' you along 'cause the longer you stay, the more he get. And you? You wastin' years waitin' on a dream that don't exist.

You keep thinkin' one day he gonna change, gonna show up as the man he promised. Girl, he already showed you who he is. This *is* the man. Ain't no future version comin'.

So stop waitin'. Stop pourin' into a bucket with a big fucking hole in the bottom. Break the damn cycle. Walk before you get drained dry. He don't need to change—you do. You need to change your perspective, change your standards, change your damn life. 'Cause the longer you let him play, the longer you stay stuck in a game that was never built for you to win.

§2.5 Keisha and Devon: The Playbook

The Slow Start – Hookin' Me Softly

Devon didn't come at me heavy. He ain't flood my mailbox with "I love yous" or promises of some fairytale future. Nah, he played it slick. First letter? Basic. Talkin' about how rough things was inside, how he missed the outside, how he was just tryna hold it together. Sounded harmless. Sounded human. And me? I ate it up. Felt sorry for him. Thought maybe he was just a misunderstood man who needed someone in his corner.

And that's how he got me. He ain't ask for money, ain't beg for nothin'—just somebody to talk to. Somebody to listen. So I wrote back. Shared my stories, opened up little pieces of myself, thinkin' we was connectin'. But what I didn't know? He wasn't just listenin'. He was studyin'.

Emotional Profilin' – How He Found My Weak Spots

See, every letter I sent was like a test I ain't know I was takin'. I thought I was bein' real, lettin' him in. But he was takin' notes. My past hurts? Logged. My insecurities? Logged. My soft spot for "helpin' people"? Logged.

He mirrored my values right back at me like he was the male version of me. I'd say I wanted to help folks, and suddenly he wished he had someone like me growin' up. I'd say I craved stability, and he start talkin' about how he wanted the same thing. Shit felt genuine. Felt like he saw me. But nah—he was shapeshiftin', reflectin' everything I said so I'd believe he was my perfect match.

That's the predator playbook, baby: figure out where you weak, then make you believe you strong together.

Mirror & Match – The Reflection Game

Let me tell you—this man was good. He mirrored me so well, I thought he was my twin flame. I'd say, *"I love my family,"* and suddenly he love family too. I'd dream out loud about a life after struggle, and guess what? He got the same damn dream.

But it wasn't real. He wasn't givin' me himself—he was givin' me me. All he did was flip my words back at me dressed up like his own. It made me feel safe, seen, like we was aligned. But really? He was just buildin' a fake version of himself outta my hopes.

The Long Game – Patience as a Weapon

That's where Devon stood out—he ain't rush. Most dudes try to cash in quick, but him? Nah, he slow-cooked me. Fed me just enough affection, just enough promises, just enough "we gonna build together" talk to keep me comin' back for more.

And patience? That was his weapon. He ain't need me to give it all up at once. He knew if he played it slow, if he let me believe we was buildin' somethin' real, I'd hand over everything piece by piece—time, energy, emotions, loyalty—without even seein' I was the only one investin'.

The Wake-Up Call

One day it hit me like a fucking brick to the face—I wasn't buildin' shit with him. I was buildin' his hustle. I was pourin' out my time, my love, my energy into a fantasy while he sat back collectin' it all, givin' me just enough to keep me hooked.

That future we talked about? Didn't exist. The house, the job, the family—all smoke. He never meant to build nothin' with me. I was a construction worker buildin' his empire while he kicked back and watched.

So I did the only thing left—I walked. Cut ties. Left his ass behind. 'Cause once you realize you been used, the worst thing you can do is keep lettin' it happen.

Keisha's Final Word

Don't let nobody run Devon's playbook on you. Recognize the slow game, the mirror game, the patience game—all of it. If a man sound too perfect, like he sayin' everything you feel in your heart? That ain't love, sis—that's strategy.

Protect your damn self. Set boundaries. See through the sweet talk. And if you feel like you startin' to lose yourself tryna save him? That's your sign to bounce. You not his savior—you just his next mark. Don't let 'em play you like they played me.

§2.6 Raven Sinclair Commentary

Addicted to the Fantasy

I've been there — chest tight, heart racing, clutching a letter like it was oxygen. I wanted every word to be real, so I convinced myself it was. "Baby, you're all I got." "Nobody ever loved me like you do." I'd sit on the edge of my bed at midnight, legs crossed, reading that shit over and over, picturing his hands on me even though he was locked in a concrete box. And yeah, sometimes it went further — I'd touch myself just to feel close to a man who wasn't even there. That's how deep the fantasy dug its claws in.

Fed Back My Own Scars

But the ugly truth? He wasn't pouring his heart out to me — he was profiling me like a cop studying a suspect. He knew my weak spots because I told him. My loneliness. My craving to be seen. My history of picking men who treated me like an afterthought. He mirrored it all back at me like he was the cure. I ate it up. Meanwhile, he was building his hustle brick by brick, making me feel needed so I'd keep feeding him what he wanted — my money, my energy, my damn body from a distance.

The nastiest part? I *knew* some of it was fake, but I wanted it anyway. That's the trap. You tell yourself, "He wouldn't waste this much time if it wasn't real." But prison men got nothing but time. He used patience like a weapon. Slow texts, long letters, just enough to keep me craving the next hit. It was addiction disguised as affection.

And when the mask slipped — when the asks started stacking, when the guilt trips slid in — I still didn't cut him off. I'd lay there staring at the ceiling, phone glowing in my hand, feeling dirty and ashamed but still answering. That's what predators count on: not just your love, but your silence. You're too embarrassed to admit how far you've gone, so you stay. And every day you stay, you bleed a little more.

The Mirror Breaks

The day I finally broke it was messy. I caught myself crying with one hand on the phone and the other still clutching a letter that smelled like his cologne. I looked at myself in the mirror and thought, *This ain't love, this is self-*

destruction. And I was done. Blocked him. Stopped writing. Walked the fuck away. It hurt like ripping off my own skin — but it was the only way I ever got free.

So here's what I need you to know: don't romanticize your own exploitation. If the love you're chasing makes you cry more than it makes you smile, if you're giving more than you're getting, if you feel drained instead of lifted — it's not love. It's a hustle. And no orgasm, no letter, no whispered "forever" is worth your soul.

§2.7 Larry Levine Commentary

Romance? Nah, You're the Food Chain

Oh, you thought this chapter was about love? Cute. Let me rip the Band-Aid off: if you're in a relationship with some dude in a cell, you're not in a Hallmark movie, you're in a fucking wildlife documentary. He's the predator, you're the prey, and the only thing missing is David Attenborough narrating while you empty your savings into his commissary.

You think he's listening to you? No, sweetheart, he's running analytics like the fucking NSA. Every trauma, every ex that cheated, every daddy issue — logged. He's not bonding, he's building a PowerPoint on how to keep you on the hook. And you hand him the data like a fool because it feels "deep." Spoiler: it's not deep, it's manipulation dressed up with sad eyes and a pencil stub.

Build-A-Bear Bullshit

And let's talk about the "future" he's selling. House, kids, dog, white picket fence. Bitch, please. The only fence in his future is barbed wire. You're out here playing Build-a-Bear with a con artist, stitching a dream together while he's jerking off in his bunk writing the same shit to four other women. And you're the one crying into your pillow thinking you're special. Newsflash: the only thing "special" about you is how quickly you volunteered to bankroll his soap opera.

The long game? That's not devotion, that's patience. Prison men got nothing but time, and they'll slow-cook you like a fucking brisket until you're tender enough to fall off the bone — aka, hand over your bank card without even questioning it. And when you finally do question it? He pulls the guilt trip, the silence, the "you're all I got" speech. And you fold, again, because your dumb ass thinks love means being a 24/7 emotional crisis hotline with a side of Western Union.

Here's the part you won't like: he's not waiting for you, he's waiting *out you*. Waiting until you're so hooked on his lies you'll do anything to keep the fantasy alive. And when he finally drops you? Don't worry, he's already got another chick lined up. It's like Uber Eats, but for desperate women with cash.

So yeah, you can keep convincing yourself you're the one who's gonna change him, heal him, save him. But the only thing you're saving is his commissary balance. If you want to get played, fine — but at least admit you signed up for it. And if you don't? Then close the fucking fairytale book, pull your head out of your ass, and stop letting some con with a ballpoint pen treat you like an ATM that moans.

CHAPTER THREE

Love Bomb Cycle

§3.1 The Emergency Trap – "I Need This for My Mom" Game

Now that they've got you hooked with the small asks, here's the switch-up: The emergency trap. This one's slick. They're not just asking for cash for themselves anymore. Now it's about family—about his mama, his sister, someone close. It's the classic "I need this for my mom's hospital bill" line, or maybe it's "My sister's in a bad spot, I gotta help her out."

They've shifted the game. Now it's not just about them. It's about someone they love, someone you can relate to. And these motherfuckers know damn well that when they pull on your heartstrings like that, you're gonna feel like you have to help. They make it about family, and who's gonna say no to that?

But here's the truth: It's all a lie. They don't care about their momma's hospital bill. They don't care about their sister's problems. They care about getting you to open your fucking wallet and keep giving. And once you've been hooked with the family emergency, it's a wrap. You're emotionally invested now, and they know it.

The Guilt Trap: Hook, Line, and Sinker

They play you with guilt. The minute you even think about not helping, they'll hit you with a fucking guilt trip: "I can't believe you'd let my mom suffer." Or, "If you really cared, you'd help." It's manipulation at its finest. They know exactly how to make you feel like the bad guy if you don't come through. And guess what? You'll end up sending the money because you don't wanna feel guilty. You'll tell yourself you're doing the right thing. You're helping. But it's all part of the hustle.

The Reality Check: The Emergency is Fake

Let me hit you with some real talk: that fake ass "emergency" is pure bullshit. They're using your compassion to manipulate you into giving. And once they know they've got your emotions tied up in their family drama, it's game over. They've got you locked in, and they're gonna keep asking for more.

They make you feel responsible for someone else's crisis, and that's how they reel you in. It starts with one emergency, but before you know it, they're hitting you with another. It's a slow burn, and by the time you realize what's going on, you're already in too deep.

Keisha's Reality Check

I've seen it. I've been there. The "emergency" is just another move in their playbook. They don't care about their mama's hospital bill. They just want to control you emotionally, make you feel like you have to help. And every time you give in, it gets easier for them to ask for more.

The second you realize you're being played, it's time to stop. You're not responsible for their family's problems. Don't fall for the guilt. Don't let these slick-ass motherfuckers play you like they played me.

Keisha's Closing Advice

When they hit you with that "I need this for my mom" crap, don't buy it. It's a hustle, girl. And you're not their emotional ATM. Stand firm. Recognize the game for what it is before they reel you in even deeper. You're not here to fix their family issues. Stop playing their game.

§3.2 – Layered Requests: From Commissary to "Fresh Starts"

Once they know you'll give, the game changes. It doesn't stay at snacks or a quick $20 for a phone card. That was the hook. Now they stack the asks like layers of concrete. First it's commissary, then it's shoes, then *"I need a little something for the lawyer."* Before long, you're covering their calls, legal fees, sneakers, even "savings" for when they get out. Piece by piece, dollar by dollar, you're building their empire while your account bleeds out.

The Illusion of Progress

Here's the slickest part: they frame every new ask like it's for a higher purpose. Not just food — but "nutrition for focus." Not just a lawyer fee — but "the chance to shave years off my sentence." Not just cash for when they hit the street — but "seed money for a new life." They're selling you hope. They're dangling this fantasy where your money is the ticket to their transformation. But that "fresh start" is bullshit. They're not planning a rebirth; they're planning their next hustle, funded by you.

The Slow Burn

Think about how it creeps. You send $20, no sweat. Next week it's $50, and you justify it: *"I've already sent some, what's a little more?"* Then it's $150 for a lawyer retainer, $200 for "reentry classes," $300 for "work clothes when I get out." Each request feels connected, logical even. That's the trap — it's never random. It's a steady climb, designed so you don't feel the slope until you're halfway up the damn mountain.

The Trap of Commitment

By now you're invested. You've already given this sorry ass romeo scammer maybe hundreds, and stopping feels like throwing it all away. That's the psychology they exploit — the sunk-cost trap. You think, *"If I don't help with this last thing, all the money I already gave is wasted."* They know that. They know once you're in deep, you'll bend further to avoid admitting you've been played. That guilt? That pride? That's their leverage.

Keisha's Reality Check

I'll give it to you raw: I've lived this. I once sent $300 thinking it was the last "lawyer fee" he'd ever need. Two weeks later, dude asked for $500 more — "for paperwork." There was no paperwork. There was no lawyer. There was just me, being played. That's the hustle — one layer stacked on another until you can't even see where it started. And by the time you wake up, you're bled dry.

Keisha's Closing Advice

Don't let the layers pile up. Every "just this once" stacks into a pattern that's hard to break. Recognize it early: lawyer fees, reentry fantasies, commissary, "fresh starts" — it's all the same play dressed different. Stop it before the cycle owns you. You're not their sponsor, their investor, or their financial planner. You're their target — unless you shut it down.

§3.3 – The Hidden Hustle: Funding the Crew Without Knowing

The Pass-Through Economy

You think you're helping *him*. Cute. What you're actually doing is fueling a mini-economy. Money goes in his account, but value moves sideways. Commissary becomes currency. Items get flipped, debts get settled, favors get purchased. That $100 you "gifted"? It didn't die in his ramen bowl—it got sliced, traded, and redistributed like you just sponsored snack time for half the block.

The Buddy System (a.k.a. Your Cash, Their Network)

It's never just one man. He's got a crew, and crews share resources. Your "for soap and calls" transfer? Magically becomes sneakers for a buddy, snack packs for a lieutenant, or buy-ins for whatever side hustle they're running. You're not his partner—you're the silent investor they forgot to tell you about.

How It Slips Past You

- **Third-party routes:** "Can you send it to my boy's girl—faster that way." Translation: covering someone else's tab with your money.
- **Stacked reasons:** This week "commissary," next week "owe my cellie," next week "we all put in." See the pattern? You're paying their group bill.
- **Weird timing:** Asks spike right before store day or right after some "incident." That's not coincidence; that's payroll.
- **Vague accounting:** Lots of "I'll show you later," zero receipts, shifting numbers. Because clarity kills the con.

Why You Don't Catch It (At First)

Because it *feels* generous. You tell yourself you're keeping him afloat. They count on that. Distance + guilt = compliance. And once you've sent a few times, the sunk-cost trap snaps shut: *"I've already helped this far, I can't stop now."* That's the leash.

What Your Money Actually Buys

Not just food. Leverage. Status. Favors. Your cash props up a tiny power structure you can't see—snacks traded for protection, shoes traded for access, "loans" floated at interest. You're underwriting a business model you never agreed to.

Keisha's Reality Check

I've watched women bankroll entire crews while believing they were "holding down their man." He wasn't struggling—he was *managing inventory*. Every dollar you send expands his reach inside. That warm feeling you get from helping? That's the product they're selling you. The margin is your bank balance.

Keisha's Closing Advice

Stop acting like the block's foundation. No third-party sends. No "owe my boy" nonsense. If it isn't specific, verifiable, and one-time, it's a no. The second your money starts moving sideways, you cut the line. You aint the bank; you are the boundary. PERIOD.

§3.4 – Chasing Devon's Lies: A Story of Giving Too Much

The Hook

It started with Devon sliding into my DMs, smooth-talking like he'd been practicing that script his whole damn life. The sob story, the "I'm just a man trying to get by" routine — I'd heard it all before. But he had that spark, that charm, that look in his eyes that made me think, *maybe this one's different.* So when he hit me with, *"Can you help me out with $20 for commissary?"* I told myself, "It's just $20. No harm." That was the first mistake.

The Escalation

The gratitude poured in, and I felt good — useful, needed. But one ask turned into another. $50 for books. $100 for phone calls. $150 for lawyer fees. Each time, I told myself, *just this once.* Each time, Devon played the role of the desperate man with nobody else in his corner. I thought I was helping. In reality, I was being conditioned. Every dollar wasn't support — it was training me to say yes again.

The Emotional Trap

He knew the lines to pull: *"You're the only one who cares about me." "I couldn't survive in here without you."* And I bought it. Not because the words were special, but because I wanted to believe them. That's the game — make you feel like the hero, like you're part of their redemption story. So when he asked for $200 "for when I get out," I didn't even blink. By then, I was too far in, emotionally and financially.

The Big Ask

Then came the $500 play: "I'll need money for rent when I get out." My stomach dropped, but I still sent it. Why? Because by that point I was chasing sunk costs, scared that saying no would erase everything I'd already given. I thought I was investing in our future. Truth was, I was just another funding source in his hustle.

The Collapse

When Devon finally got out, I expected gratitude, a reunion, maybe even a life we'd talked about. What I got was the same man, the same lies, the same endless asks. Nothing changed. The promises were smoke. I wasn't a partner in his future — I was the ATM that financed his past. That night, staring at the numbers in my bank account and the lies in my inbox, it hit me: I'd been played. Every "I love you," every promise, every tearful story — all part of the hustle.

Keisha's Reality Check

You can't save a man who doesn't want to be saved. You can't love someone into changing. And you sure as hell can't buy your way into a real relationship. I let my emotions blind me, thinking my money could build his future. But all it did was pad his hustle. When I finally cut him off, it hurt like hell — but it gave me my power back.

Keisha's Closing Advice

Here's the takeaway: the game always starts small, but it ends with you drained. Don't chase the fantasy. Don't believe that one more transfer will make him change. When you feel yourself getting pulled into the cycle, stop.

Protect your wallet, protect your energy, protect yourself. Because once you're the bank, you're no longer the partner — you're just the mark.

§3.5 Raven Sinclair's Commentary

The Price of Playing Savior

I don't care how many times you dress it up with "it's for my mom," "it's just commissary," or "this is the last thing I'll ever ask" — I've seen the game. I've lived the game. And I bled for it. You think you're helping a man survive, but you're actually helping him build a damn empire on your back.

I've wired money in the middle of the night with my stomach knotted, telling myself it was love. I've answered those guilt-soaked calls where he made me feel like if I didn't come through, his whole world would collapse. And guess what? Nothing collapsed except my bank account and my self-respect.

Training Him to Use You

Here's the part most women don't wanna hear: every time you send that cash, you're training him. You think you're showing love, but you're teaching him exactly how far he can push you. He learns what button makes you fold, what lie makes you reach for your debit card. And once he knows the combo? He'll punch it every damn time until you're tapped out.

And let's not pretend it's just him. Half the time your "help" ain't even helping him — it's helping the crew. You send money thinking you're feeding your man, but really you're feeding a whole block of hustlers you don't even know exist. That $100 you thought bought him shoes? It bought three other dudes' commissary and a stack of honey buns.

Cutting the Line Before It Cuts You

The ugliest part? I knew. Deep down, I knew. When the asks stacked higher and the excuses got thinner, my gut screamed. But I stayed. Because leaving meant admitting I'd been used. And that shame kept me chained longer than his lies ever did.

So let me be blunt: stop playing savior. Stop paying "family bills" for people you never met. Stop believing the guilt trips, the layered asks, the "last time, I swear." If his emergencies are endless, if his needs keep multiplying, if you feel more like an ATM than a woman — that's because you are.

You don't fix this cycle by giving more. You fix it by cutting the line, even if it hurts like hell. Because the only "emergency" here is how fast you're letting him strip you bare.

§3.6 Larry Levine Commentary

FEMA With Lip Gloss

Let's quit bullshitting — you weren't "helping his family," you were running a goddamn disaster relief fund with your name on it. Except FEMA sends water and blankets, and you're out here sending Western Union slips to a guy crying about his mama's fake hospital bill. Newsflash: his mom ain't sick, his sister ain't broke, and his grandma ain't coughing up blood — but your bank account sure the fuck is. You weren't his angel; you were his Red Cross with tits. And he knew every time he said "baby, if you really cared," your dumb ass would melt like butter and hit "send."

Shark Tank for Suckers

This is the part I love — watching women bankroll some fool's entire fantasy empire like they're investors on Shark Tank. Only difference? Mark Cuban doesn't cry when you say no. This guy stacks bullshit on top of bullshit until you're bleeding money like a casino slot machine. First it's ramen, then it's sneakers, then it's "lawyer fees," and before you know it, you're paying for a "fresh start fund" while he's laughing his ass off trading your Oreos for blowjobs in the shower. You weren't a partner — you were a fucking donor. Congratulations, you just became the silent investor in *Honey Bun Enterprises, LLC.*

ATM With a Soul

Here's where it gets dark — you stopped being his girlfriend and turned into his personal ATM. And not even a normal ATM. No — you're the deluxe version that apologizes for not spitting out twenties fast enough. Every time you said "no," he pulled out the guilt trip: "You're all I got, baby, don't let me down." And you folded. Over and over. Like clockwork. And while you were crying into your pillow, telling yourself "I'm the one who understands him," he was in his cell running the exact same lines on two other women who were also playing Florence Nightingale with their debit cards. You weren't chosen, you were rotated. You weren't his queen, you were his utility bill with pussy.

So yeah, keep telling yourself you're "building a future" with him. Meanwhile, he's building a commissary empire on your dime and laughing about it with his crew. At some point, sweetheart, you don't need "true love" — you need a helmet, because you're running headfirst into a brick wall called *reality*.

CHAPTER FOUR

Guardrails Ain't Weakness

§4.1 – Guilt Trips & Silent Treatment

The Setup: Emotional Handcuffs

Lemme break it down for you — prison dudes don't need fists to fuck you up. They'll chain your mind instead. First play out the gate? The guilt trip. That's when everything — and I mean everything — somehow becomes your fault. Didn't hit Western Union this week? *"Damn, I see you don't really care about me like I thought."* Didn't answer your phone 'cause you were at work? *"Guess I ain't important enough for you."* Bitch, please. That ain't love, that's manipulation with a side of cheap theatrics.

See, guilt works because you're wired to fix shit. You're sitting there thinking, *"I don't wanna hurt him, he's already locked up, he's suffering enough."* He knows this. He milks that. Suddenly, you're not the girlfriend — you're the damn therapist, crisis hotline, and emergency bank teller rolled into one. And every time you fold, he clocks it as a win.

The Freeze-Out: Silent Treatment Games

When guilt don't break you fast enough, they ice you out. That's the second weapon. Silence. No texts, no calls, no love notes. Dead air like he fell off the earth. And now you're trippin'. *"Did I say something wrong? Did I push him too far? What the hell did I do?"* Girl, you did nothing. That's the trick.

They want you spinning. They want you pacing your apartment like a dumbass fiend chasing a fix, checking your phone every five minutes, feeling like you gotta fix it. That's the chokehold. And once you break? Once you send that *"Hey, are you okay? Did I do something?"* text? Boom. Hooked again. He knows you'll chase. And if he can get you chasing silence, he can get you chasing anything.

The Emotional Rollercoaster: Guilt, Silence, Repeat

This ain't random. It's a cycle. They'll guilt you until you cave, then vanish until you panic. Back and forth until you're dizzy. It's like being on a ride you never wanted a ticket for — except this rollercoaster don't end. And here's the killer: the more you chase, the deeper they pull you in. You're not "fixing" the relationship, you're proving you'll run laps for their approval.

I seen women send hundreds, even thousands, just to "make it right" after a silent stretch. I knew a girl who missed one phone call 'cause she was at work — dude iced her for a week. She begged him back with a $250 GreenDot card, like that was some love offering. That's not a relationship. That's a fucking ransom.

Keisha's Reality Check

Let me slap you with the truth: if a man's running guilt trips and silence on you, you're not his queen — you're his puppet. He's pulling strings, and you're dancing. Ain't no respect in that, ain't no love in that, and sure as hell ain't no future in that. It's control. It's game. Straight up.

Keisha's Closing Advice

 So here's the rule, and tattoo this on your forehead if you have to: Don't chase silence. Don't apologize for crimes you didn't commit. Don't bend when you ain't even the one in the wrong. If he can't talk to you like an adult without flipping your feelings into weapons, then he don't deserve your time, your money, or your damn energy. Walk away before you're bled dry and left wondering why the hell you ever thought this was love.

§4.2 – Jealousy Traps

The Setup: Planting Seeds in Your Head

Girl, jealousy is their favorite drug, and they'll feed it to you in doses till you're high off suspicion. They drop little crumbs, like, *"Oh yeah, I heard from Janine today,"* or *"My homegirl Tanya always looks out for me."* Sounds harmless, right? Nah, that's the hook. They know exactly how that shit hits. Suddenly you're sitting there, stomach knotted, wondering: *"What's she got that I don't? Why he even mentioning her to me?"* And the second you start spinning, you're in the trap. They don't even gotta cheat for real — just make you think about it. They plant the doubt, then sit back and watch you sweat.

The Fire: They Eat Off Your Reactions

Here's the part that stings — they want you mad. They want you jealous. Every time you roll your eyes, every time you blow up their phone, every time you start snapping about *"Who the hell is Janine?"* — they're eating that shit up like fucking popcorn. That's proof to them you're locked in, you're emotionally invested, you're fighting for their attention. And don't get it twisted, this ain't random. It's calculated. They'll bring up some "friend" just to see if you'll bite. And when you do? Jackpot. Now they know you'll compete for their scraps.

The Hidden Message: Control, Not Love

Understand this: it ain't about the other women. Half the time, that "ex" or "friend" barely exists in the way he says. It's about control. He wants you insecure, always questioning yourself, always working harder to prove you're the one. If you're too busy chasing validation, you can't see the hustle for what it is. And he knows it. That's why he keeps you dangling — a little attention here, a mention of some other woman there — like a carrot on a string. You chase, he controls. Simple math.

The Long Con: Draining You With Insecurity

This game don't stop. Once he clocks that jealousy works on you, it's a button he'll push forever. Today it's Janine. Tomorrow it's *"some chick from the block who always looks out."* Next week it's an *"old friend"* who popped back up. You'll be chasing ghosts while he's sitting back, watching you twist yourself in knots. And the more jealous you get, the more you give — more time, more energy, sometimes more money — trying to prove you're the one. Meanwhile, he's running the same play on the next woman, laughing at how easy it is to keep y'all fighting shadows.

Keisha's Reality Check

Listen, I grew up around this bullshit, and I've lived it too. Ain't nothing special about these jealousy games — it's recycled hustle. He don't care about Janine. He don't care about Tanya. He don't even care if you lose your damn mind over it. What he cares about is knowing he can yank your strings anytime he feels like it. If you're constantly competing, constantly proving, constantly begging for the top spot, you ain't his queen — you're just another sorry-ass contestant.

Keisha's Closing Advice

Don't play that game. If he's got you feeling like you're in competition, step back and recognize the hustle. Real love ain't about making you jealous just to test if you care. That's manipulation, plain and simple. Don't let anybody drag you into proving your worth while they sit back like a prize to be won. You're not a contestant. You're not an option. And the second you see those jealousy traps getting laid out, that's your cue to dip. Keep your crown on straight, stop chasing shadows, and leave him in the dirt where he belongs.

§4.3 – The Hero Save

The Setup: Break You, Then Bandage You

Girl, this one right here is the dirtiest trick in the book. After they've run you through guilt trips, iced you out with silence, or got you spinnin' jealous over some imaginary "Janine," here comes the big performance: the hero save. That's when they slither back all lovey-dovey, like nothing ever happened. They come in hot with *"I love you, baby, you're all I got"* like they ain't just left you drowning in doubt for a week. They'll hold you, whisper how much they missed you, act like they're the only one who truly understands you. And because you're drained as hell from the fight, you let it slide. You eat it up, thinking, *"Finally, we're back on track."* Nah, girl — that's just them resetting the game so they can run it again.

The Emotional Hook: Feeding You What You Crave

They know exactly when to pounce. They leave you starved for affection, then flood you with it when you're weakest. That's why it feels so damn good when they finally show up sweet. They built that drought on purpose so they could sell you the rain. It's not real love — it's love-bombing. A performance. They're not "saving" you, they're keeping you addicted. And every time you fall for it, you're training yourself to forgive faster, chase harder, and settle deeper into the leash they've got around your neck.

The Cycle: Push, Pull, Repeat

This ain't a one-off. This is a cycle they run until you either snap out of it or get drained dry. Step one: push you away with coldness, blame, or jealousy games.

Step two: vanish long enough for you to doubt yourself, beg, or stew. Step three: come back with hugs, "I missed you," and promises of forever. You melt, forget the bullshit, and think maybe this time it's real. Then the wheel starts spinning all over again. It's psychological warfare dressed up like romance. And the longer you ride it, the more dependent you get — until you believe you need them just to feel whole. That's the trap.

The Dependency Scam: Why It Works

See, girl, the real hustle ain't just the affection — it's the dependency. They want you convinced they're the only one who can make you feel loved. That's power. That's leverage. And when you buy into it, you'll forgive anything. You'll overlook lies, ignore red flags, send more money, because you're hooked on that "hero save" high. They created the wound just so they could sell you the bandage. That ain't love, that's straight-up manipulation on steroids.

Keisha's Reality Check

Let me give it to you raw: I've been that fool, waiting by the phone, crying into my pillow, then melting when he finally came back sweet-talking. It ain't romance — it's manipulation on crack. They don't want partnership, they want dominance. They don't want love, they want a puppet. And every time you let the "hero save" slide, you hand them the strings to pull.

Keisha's Closing Advice

Recognize the damn pattern. If somebody disappears, wrecks your peace, then strolls back acting like your savior, that ain't your man — that's your manipulator. Don't let the fake tenderness trick you into forgetting the pain they caused. Walk before you get played into believing chaos is love. Consistency is love. Respect is love. All this push-pull "hero save" nonsense? That's just another hustle in their arsenal. Don't fall for it.

§4.4 – Charm in the Streets, Control in the Sheets

The Setup: Mr. Perfect on Display

Girl, let's call this what it is — the two-faced hustle. Out in public, he's smooth as silk. Holding your hand, whispering sweet shit in your ear, making sure everybody sees he's got himself a queen. He'll brag about how lucky he is, look you dead in the eye like you're his whole damn world. To the crowd, y'all are #RelationshipGoals. People start telling you how good you've got it, how they wish they had a man like him. And you believe it. You think, *"Damn, maybe I really hit the jackpot."*

That's the act. That's the show. And you're the co-star whether you signed up or not.

The Switch: Behind Closed Doors

Now cut the lights, close the door, and see what happens. That charming prince? Gone. The love bombing dries up, and the real him slithers out. Suddenly it's cold shoulders, gaslighting, and guilt trips. You're not his queen anymore, you're the punching bag for his control issues. He'll twist your words, flip every argument back on you, and leave you questioning your own damn sanity. One minute he's kissing your hand in front of his homies, the next he's telling you you're nothing without him. That ain't romance — that's some bait-and-switch bullshit.

The Illusion: Why You Stay Hooked

Here's why it works — because when the world sees Mr. Perfect, you start doubting yourself. Everyone's like, *"He's such a good guy, you're lucky to have him,"* and you think maybe the problem really is you. That's the illusion. He's smart enough to keep the mask shiny in public, so when he tears you down in private, nobody believes your side. You end up second-guessing yourself, thinking maybe you just need to try harder, be better, love him more. Meanwhile, he's running circles around you — charming the streets, controlling the sheets.

The Double Standard: His Image vs Your Reality

Understand this: he don't give a damn about you feeling safe or valued. What he cares about is how the world sees him. As long as people think he's a great boyfriend, he gets to keep treating you like trash behind the scenes. He's not protecting you, he's protecting his reputation. That's the scam. Public charm keeps you from walking, private control keeps you in check.

Keisha's Reality Check

Girl, I grew up around this game, and I've lived it. Let me tell you: if his sweetness has an audience, but his cruelty only shows up when you're alone, you ain't with a man, you're with a manipulator. Real love don't flip like a light switch. Real love is consistent — in front of friends, in front of family, and when it's just the two of you. If he's gotta perform for the streets and then break you down behind closed doors, that's not love. That's a con.

Keisha's Closing Advice

Don't get fooled by the mask. If you're being treated like a queen in public but like shit in private, the public version ain't real — the private one is. Recognize the game before you lose yourself trying to keep up the illusion he built. Don't stick around just 'cause everybody else thinks you're the "perfect couple." They ain't living your reality. Walk away. You deserve love that's steady, not love that's staged.

§4.5 Raven Sinclair Commentary

The Puppet Strings You Don't See

I remember when I first fell for that guilt trip shit — every missed call felt like a crime, every "where were you?" had me apologizing like I murdered someone. That's the trap: you start thinking you're responsible for his happiness. Nah, baby — that's his circus, not yours. What he's doing is stringing you up like a marionette, making you dance every time he pouts. And the silence? That's worse. That's the choke chain. You'll damn near lose your mind pacing the floor, checking your phone, replaying conversations. I've been there, heart racing, stomach twisted, asking myself, *"What the hell did I do?"* Truth? Nothing. That's the game — he builds the storm, then sells you the umbrella.

Competing With Ghosts

Jealousy is a slow poison, and I've swallowed it before. One "homegirl" mentioned, one "friend" from the past, and suddenly I was out here spiraling, wondering if I wasn't enough. That's the design. He wants you questioning, doubting, proving yourself harder each time. And it works — you catch yourself putting in extra energy, bending over backwards, fighting invisible women that don't even exist. I've lived that humiliation — the sleepless nights, the angry texts, the sick feeling in my chest like I was losing a competition I never signed up for. The worst part? He fed off it. My jealousy wasn't a problem to him; it was proof I was hooked. And that's when I learned the hard way: if a man can make you fight for scraps, he's already stripped you of your crown.

Love Ain't Supposed to Hurt This Way

Here's what finally snapped me out of it: realizing the "hero save" and the public act were all part of the same damn show. He'd break me down with guilt, freeze me out with silence, drive me mad with jealousy — then swoop back in with hugs, whispers, and promises, like I should be grateful he even showed up. And in public? Mr. Perfect. Smiling, holding my hand, calling me his queen while everyone clapped for our "love story." Meanwhile, behind closed doors I was gutted, doubting myself, carrying scars nobody else could see. That's not love. That's a con dressed up in roses. Real love don't flip-flop depending on who's watching. Real love don't turn you into a puppet, a contestant, or a patient in need of constant saving.

So here's my bottom line, girl: guardrails ain't weakness, they're survival. If you let a man chain your emotions with guilt, silence, and jealousy, he'll have you living in chaos and calling it love. Don't play that game. Protect your peace like your life depends on it — because it does.

§4.6 Larry Levine Commentary

The Pity Olympics You'll Never Win

Let's cut the crap — if you're out here apologizing for missing a call because you were *working to pay his bills*, you've officially entered the Pity Olympics. And guess what? You're not even on the podium. You're the sucker in the stands buying tickets. These motherfuckers weaponize guilt like it's a goddamn sport. "If you really cared…" *Cue the violins*. Meanwhile, you're bending over backwards to fix problems you didn't create. He doesn't need a girlfriend; he needs a full-time therapist with a side hustle as a loan officer. You think you're loving him? No — you're underwriting his bullshit. And the worst part? You're doing it voluntarily.

Jealousy: His Favorite Porn Category

This one kills me. Women tearing themselves apart over *ghost bitches* he sprinkles into conversation like seasoning. "Janine said hi." Boom — now you're losing sleep, stalking Facebook profiles, wondering if you're enough.

Hate to break it to you, but you're not competing with Janine. You're competing with his need to see you unravel. That's the kink. That's the porn. Your insecurity is his hard-on. And while you're fighting shadows, guess what? He's running the same play on another woman, getting off on the same jealousy drip-feed. You're not his queen. You're his entertainment.

Chaos Ain't Love, It's Leverage

Here's where I stop playing nice: if you're sitting there crying because Mr. Perfect in public turned into Mr. Asshole in private, then congratulations — you've been drafted into the emotional hunger games. The guilt trips, the silent treatment, the "hero save," the charm show — all of it is one giant loop designed to make you chase stability that doesn't fucking exist. And every time you forgive, every time you beg, every time you stay? That's leverage he'll cash in later. Real love doesn't hold you hostage. Real love doesn't flip-flop like a light switch. This shit ain't love — it's control dressed up in roses and hashtags.

So here's the Levine takeaway: if you're still buying into this cycle after reading all this, you don't need a man — you need a helmet. Because you're running headfirst into the same brick wall over and over, then crying about the concussion. Guardrails ain't weakness, sweetheart — they're survival. Build some, or get used to being roadkill.

The Playbook Unfolds

What These Modules Cover

Welcome back to the grind. Module 1 showed you the bait; Module 2 is the goddamn instruction manual. This is the part where you finally realize he ain't stumbling through this — he's running plays like a seasoned hustler with a whistle and a playbook.

CHAPTER 5 – The Forever Lie

You're not "the one," you're a slot on his roster. Texas chick sends stamps, Ohio chick pays phone bills, you send snacks. Fake "sisters" and "family" pop up to cover his hustle. And your pics and letters? Flipped into prison currency before the ink's dry.

CHAPTER 6 – The Hustler's Toolbox:

His words ain't romance, they're scripts. Mirroring, gaslighting, guilt-trips, silence — all sharpened tools. He feeds you highs like a dealer, then starves you till you chase. Closure is bullshit; silence is the only clean break.

CHAPTER 7 – The Isolation Game

Devon wasn't love, he was the lesson. He made me bend my schedule, drain my wallet, and drown in fantasy. It wasn't him I was hooked on — it was the dream of him. When the cracks showed, I walked cold. No speeches, no goodbyes — just gone.

CHAPTER 8 – Why Real Love is Rare

Real love in this game is like unicorns on crack — technically possible, practically extinct. If it costs you money, sanity, or respect, it's not love. Guardrails aren't cold, they're survival. Without them, you're not a partner, you're livestock.

The Real Takeaway

This ain't about forever, it's about funding. Module 2 proves these dudes don't want wives, they want wages. They don't build futures, they build fantasies. The second you confuse being chosen with being cherished, you're already the mark. Bottom line: if it looks like a hustle, feels like a hustle, and empties your bank account like a hustle? Congratulations, you've been hustled.

CHAPTER FIVE

The Forever Lie

§5.1 – Multiple Pen Pals: You Ain't the Only One, Girl

The Setup: Welcome to the Roster

Girl, let's quit the fairy tale shit — you ain't the only one. That man is sittin' in his bunk running lines like a DJ spinning old records. He's got women coast to coast thinking they're "the one." Texas chick thinks she's his soulmate, you're the "ride-or-die," and some lady in Ohio swears she's his future wife. He's not choosing — he's stacking. You're not the prize, you're a damn fucking slot on his roster.

The Plate-Spinning Hustle

He plays it like a waiter with too many tables. Monday he drops you a letter, Tuesday he slides into another inbox, Wednesday he's blowing smoke at Woman C. It ain't original either — it's copy-and-paste game. Same *"baby, you're my world"* script, different name penciled in. He knows all he needs to do is sprinkle just enough affection to keep you dangling, but never so much you catch on.

Keeping Notes Like It's a Business

The slick ones? They keep binders like accountants. Birthdays, kids' names, favorite foods — all written down like you're a client file. You think he remembered your dog's name 'cause he loves you? Nah, sis, he's got it jotted down next to three other women's favorite colors. He don't love you — he's managing you. You're not special, you're just another sorry-ass line item in his portfolio.

Multiple Streams of Income

Real hustlers know never to depend on one source of cash. Woman A short this week? No sweat, Woman B will come through. Woman B tight with her money? Woman C got her tax refund and is ready to "support her man." He spreads it out like stocks — diversified, baby. You're not love, you're liquidity.

The Overlap Game

It gets grimier. That Valentine's card you sent? Stamps bought by another woman. The snacks you funded? Shared with his crew while he's writing another chick about how lonely he is. You're not providing for him, you're funding the whole operation. That's the joke — y'all are unknowingly co-sponsoring the same hustle.

The "She's Just a Friend" Defense

Call him out and he'll hit you with the classics:

- *"She's like a sister to me."*
- *"That's just my friend from back in the day."*
- *"You're the only one I want."*

Meanwhile that "sister" is sending him $75 a month and lingerie Polaroids. That "friend"? She's stacking up his commissary. And you? You're buying the lie 'cause you want to believe you're the only one.

Why You Don't See It

You're on the outside playing by free-world rules. No Instagram to snoop, no mutual friends spilling tea. He controls the narrative completely. Letters, calls, visits — all filtered through his script. You're not getting truth, you're getting a performance, and you can't fact-check a damn thing.

The Ride-or-Die Delusion

This one cuts deep. I've seen women throw fists over a man they've never even touched outside prison walls. *"Oh, but my man's different."* No, he's not. That "connection" you swear nobody understands? Five other women got the same story, the same words, the same exact promises. Y'all are fighting over who gets played better.

The Slip-Up

The cracks always show. Maybe he slips and writes the wrong name in your letter. Maybe he sends you a picture some other chick paid for. Or maybe some woman hits your inbox with, *"Hey girl, we need to talk about our man."* And that's when it hits — you're not special, you're just the next contestant in a scam that's been running long before you got there.

Keisha's Reality Check

Here's the real question you gotta ask yourself: if you're really his one and only, why does he need more? Why are his letters recycled, why do his stories sound rehearsed, why does it all feel too damn familiar? Because it is. You're part of a rotation. You're not the exception, you're the routine.

Keisha's Closing Advice

Stop letting some dude behind bars treat you like a direct deposit. If he's juggling women like bills, don't compete — cut yourself loose. Love ain't copy-paste, and if he's making you prove you're the "real one," he's already proven you're not.

§5.2 – Fake Family: When His "Sister's" Really His Cellie

The Setup: Meet the Family That Ain't Family

Girl, if you ever get that 2 a.m. text from some "sister" talking about *"He told me how much he loves you, he just needs a little help right now"* — let me stop you there. That ain't his sister. That's a hustle. They trot out "family" 'cause they know you'll swallow it. Family equals trust, right? Wrong. That's his built-in cover story so you don't question why money's being asked in his name. He's not protecting you — he's protecting his hustle.

The Cellmate Relay System

Here's how the scam really runs: he don't even have to hit you directly. He gets his cellie's girl, his homeboy's wife, or some other chick in the mix to pose as "family." That way, when she comes at you saying *"I'm his sister, he didn't even ask me to reach out,"* it feels legit. You think it's noble, unselfish, urgent. Straight-up bullshit. He scripted that shit. You're just another mark on their tag-team relay.

The Social Media Smoke Show

The bolder ones take it digital. Fake "sister" profiles pop up on Facebook with stolen selfies and stock photos of family cookouts. "Cousins," "aunties," even fake-ass "family reunions." They'll add you, post sweet throwbacks, even interact with other girlfriends to keep it looking real. Meanwhile, every DM is just another funnel back to the commissary fund. That's not family — that's Photoshop with a hustle attached.

Why It Works So Well

t works because you want it to. You wanna believe you're the hero who stepped in when family needed backup. It feels righteous. Noble. Like you're doing something bigger than just sending cash. And he's counting on that. Family equals sacred. Family equals no questions asked. But the reality? You're funding his fraud while he sits back with clean hands.

The "Unbiased" Lie

And here's the nastiest trick: he makes "family" the mouthpiece so it looks unbiased. Like they're neutral. Like they're just looking out for him 'cause he's too proud to ask. Newsflash: that "sister" you're talking to? Might be another chick he's gaming. She thinks she's helping too, when really she's running interference for his hustle. Y'all are pawns in the same damn play, and he's the one dealing the cards.

The Slip-Ups That Expose It

Pay attention and the mask will crack. "Sis" forgets his middle name. She gives a backstory that don't match what he told you. Or worse — she lets something slip like *"When we were locked up together."* Hold up — how the hell his sister locked up with him? That's the moment you realize the whole thing's scripted. Problem is, by then, you've probably already dropped hundreds into the pot.

The Safety Net Scam

Sometimes, it ain't even about him getting the money right away. They'll stash it with "family" as a back-up fund. That way, if you cut him off tomorrow, he's still good for snacks and smokes for weeks. And when you bring it up later? He'll act shocked, embarrassed, say, *"I never asked for that, my sister crossed a line."* Meanwhile, Sis is laughing her ass off with your cash.

Keisha's Reality Check

Let me keep it all the way gutter: that "family" blowing up your phone ain't family. They're part of the scam. He's the puppet master, they're the actors, and you're the audience paying for the show. This ain't loyalty, this ain't love — this is organized emotional manipulation designed to squeeze every dollar outta you.

Keisha's Closing Advice

Don't fall for the family act. If you've never met them, never seen receipts they're real, and they only show up when money's on the line? Cut it off. Don't send a dime. Stop being their ATM dressed up as a "girlfriend." Family don't use you as a bank account. Hustlers do.

§5.3 – Online Dating Inside: Catfishing From a Concrete Jungle

Phones Behind Bars: The Real Gateway Drug

Girl, commissary don't mean shit once a man gets a phone. That's the real gold mine. With one swipe, he ain't trapped behind those walls no more — he's running game in your world. Facebook, Instagram, POF, Tinder — he's got 'em all lit up, working the apps when the block's quiet or the guards are sleeping. He ain't scrolling for fun either — every woman he talks to is a potential deposit, a walking Western Union.

Two Flavors of Hustlers: The "Prince" vs. the Catfish

- **The Pen-Pal Prince.** This clown puts his real name on pen-pal sites with a half-decent photo and a sob story like: *"Looking for friendship, someone to believe in me."* Or *"Trying to change my life, just need a queen to ride with me."* He ain't trying to hide prison — he's flipping it into bait. He knows the type who responds: women who wanna rescue somebody. He plays vulnerable, sprinkles *"good morning, beautiful"* texts like confetti, and waits till you're emotionally invested before the money asks start.

- **The Full-On Catfish.** This one's dirtier. He steals pics off random dudes' IG accounts — maybe a soldier, maybe a fitness model — then builds a whole-ass fake life around it. He's *"military overseas"* or *"offshore working"* — always some job that explains why he can't video chat. His hustle is urgency. He'll tell you exactly what you want to hear, gas you up, and once you're hooked, he reels you in for "help." That ain't romance, that's a straight-up fucking con.

Your Pictures in the Mix

Here's the part that makes me sick: your own selfies might be getting flipped into bait. That heart-emoji pic you sent? Cropped and sent to another woman. Maybe he tells her, *"This is my ex, she still won't leave me alone."* Or worse — he pretends to be you, running a whole fake lesbian romance to pull in another mark. You think you're building a relationship, but really? You're part of the lure for his next victim.

Running the Rotation

Don't get it twisted — he ain't working one profile, he's running an operation:

- One Facebook for "family.
- One legit pen-pal ad for the women who know he's locked up.
- Two or three fake dating profiles for the women who don't.
- A couple Instagrams for that "edgy bad boy" vibe.

And he's got it down to a science. That *"good morning, gorgeous"* text? It didn't just hit your phone. Seven other women got the same line five minutes apart. You're not his queen. You're part of his copy-paste assembly line.

The Scam Layer You Don't See

The women who know he's in prison? They get lines like:

- *"I just need a little help till I get on my feet."*
- *"I'm building for us, but it's hard in here."*

The women who don't know? Different script:

- *"My camera's broken."*
- *"I'm moving soon, then we'll meet."*
- *"I'm saving up for a new phone."*

He's got excuses locked and loaded for every situation. If you bounce? No problem. There's always another woman already in the queue.

Business Model, Not Love Story

Don't kid yourself — this ain't romance, it's revenue. He don't care about "forever," he cares about multiple income streams. A little from Woman A, a chunk from Woman B, emotional labor from Woman C. It's diversified like stocks. If you cut him off, he doesn't lose — he replaces you.

How to Spot the Play

- He goes dark for hours, then floods you with messages like he's catching up.
- His friends list? Random women scattered across the country.
- His stories are vague as hell, could fit anybody.
- He dodges video, dodges details, always keeps it surface-level.

Girl, if you've never met his people, never seen him in person, never verified anything beyond his texts? Wake up. You're in the rotation.

The Cold Truth

You wanna think you're special. But if you haven't seen his face in real time, touched his hand across a table, or met his family? You're not the exception. You're just one more profile in his playbook. When he's done squeezing what he needs, he'll move to the next. Love don't look like vague stories and recycled lines. That's business. And the business is you.

§5.4 – Prison Marketplace: Selling Your Pics to Other Inmates

Girl, You're the Plug and Don't Even Know It

You think you're sending love. Nah, baby, you're sending inventory. In prison, every damn thing from the outside is currency: your selfies, your lipstick-smeared letters, your $75 packages. And your "man"? He ain't stashing that under his pillow. He's flipping it like stock. That lingerie pic? Fucking gold on the yard. That handwritten poem? Premium trade. Those Oreos you paid $2 for? Tripled in value by the time they hit the tier. You're not a girlfriend — you're his damn supplier.

The Currency Exchange You'll Never See

Inside, it don't run on cash, it runs on commissary and favors. Sexy pics? Top-tier currency — worth tuna, coffee, even protection. Romantic letters? They're clout — proof he's got women on deck. Packages? Wholesale inventory. Your hoodie, your snacks, your toiletries? All flipped at three times the value. You're sending love, but he's building an economy.

The Trade Game: From Your Hands to Half the Block

That "private" selfie you sent? Shown to his cellie in exchange for honey buns. Your heartfelt letter? Read out loud like slam poetry on the tier. Your care package? Broken down and sold off piece by piece. He keeps a little, sure, but most of it? Gone before you even get your next call. You thought you were feeding him. You were stocking shelves for his hustle.

The "Send More, Baby" Play

Pay attention to the lines: *"That last pic got me through the week."* Or *"Make this one special, I'll keep it forever."* Sweet, right? Don't buy it. Every time you send something "special," you just reloaded his supply. He ain't treasuring it — he's trading it.

The Middleman Cover-Up

Sometimes he won't even move the goods himself. He'll pass 'em off so he can look innocent. Then when you ask, he swears, *"Baby, I'd never sell what you give me."* Technically true — but the middleman already did, and he got his cut. That's how he keeps his halo shiny while still running the market.

Why They Do It

It's simple:

- Money without begging. Packages = commissary stacked.
- Power. Goods buy loyalty and favors.
- Leverage. He can settle debts or buy protection with your love.

This ain't romance — it's a fucking enterprise. And in enterprise, you're just a resource.

The Reach: Once It's Gone, It's Gone

Your pic? Passed around more than a deck of cards in a poker game. Your letter? Read by dudes you'll never meet. Your Oreos? Flipped three times before canteen day. And you'll never know, 'cause he'll never tell you. That "safe and special" thing you sent? Already part of the prison economy.

The Twisted Upgrade: Selling It Outside

Some don't stop at the yard. They'll flip your pics for outside cash — CashApp, prepaid cards, you name it. That lingerie shot might not just be prison currency — it could be paying some chick's rent out here.

Keisha's Wrap-Up – Straight, No Chaser

This is the hustle, girl:

- Every woman = a revenue stream.
- Every letter = marketing material.
- Every package = wholesale stock.
- Every pic = premium currency.

Red flags? Holes in his stories, random "friends" hitting your inbox, constant begging for "special" pics or bigger packages. If you think you're the only one, you're not. You're part of a pipeline, and your love is the raw product. Once it's in the system, it's gone. No refunds, no loyalty, no respect. Just trade, sell, and brag.

And if that don't make your blood boil? Then girl, you ain't paying attention.

§5.5 Raven Sinclair Reflections

Living on a Roster, Not a Pedestal

I used to think being "the one" meant something. That if a man wrote me every day, remembered my birthday, or whispered promises about our future, I was special. But in this game? Special don't exist. You're not on a pedestal, you're on a roster. I've seen the binders — notes on favorite colors, kids' names, your damn dog's birthday. It ain't love, it's logistics.

You're not his soulmate, you're one of many deposits keeping his commissary fat. And the cruelest part? He never slips because he cares — he slips because juggling too many women makes the act messy. That "wrong name" in a letter? That ain't a mistake, it's a crack in the performance.

Family Ain't Family When It's Scripted

I fell for the "sister" routine once. She hit me up all kind, talking about how proud she was that I loved him, how much he needed me. And I wanted to believe it. Wanted to believe I was part of something bigger, a family that had my back. But family don't pop up only when money's on the line. Family don't ask for Western Union like it's Sunday collection. That "sis" wasn't his blood — she was part of the hustle, running plays while I felt righteous for helping. Looking back, I laugh at the audacity. But at the time? I cried. Because I thought I was being let into his world, when really I was just another mark standing in line with my wallet open.

Love Letters, Selfies, and Lies for Sale

The deepest cut came later, when I learned my letters and pictures weren't mine anymore. That poem I wrote? Read out loud like entertainment on the tier. That private selfie? Passed around for honey buns. I thought I was giving him intimacy, but I was just supplying inventory for his little prison marketplace. And the worst part? Some women don't find out until their pictures end up outside, flipped for real cash. That's not just betrayal — that's theft of your soul dressed up like affection.

The Reflection That Hurts

Here's the truth I wish I'd seen earlier: the forever he sells is just another product. Every "good morning, beautiful," every "one day we'll build together," every "you're the only one" is bait. He doesn't want you, he wants the rotation. He doesn't love you, he loves the supply chain. And if you don't pull back, you'll end up financing not just his hustle, but the illusion he sells to ten other women just like you.

So when you catch yourself thinking, *"I'm different, I'm the one"* — stop. Ask yourself why a man who loves you needs so many backups, so many scripts, so many lies. Because if he did, you wouldn't be part of the Forever Lie — you'd be living a truth that doesn't require explanation.

§5.6 Larry Levine Reflections

Congratulations, You're on the Farm Team

Let's get this outta the way — you weren't the starter, you weren't the MVP, and you sure as fuck weren't "the one." You were in the lineup, right there with six other women, all running the same plays. He's not whispering love letters to you like you're Juliet. He's copy-pasting the same script with different names slotted in like a mad lib. "Baby, you're my world." Really? Your world must be crowded as hell if it's got five pen pals, a "sister," and two catfish profiles living in it. You're not special, sweetheart. You're a stock option in his portfolio, and the dividends are ramen, stamps, and GreenDot cards.

Family Reunion My Ass

If some random "sister" or "cousin" hits you up at 2 a.m. with sob stories about how much he loves you and just needs "a little help" — congratulations, you've just been baptized into the Church of Bullshit. That ain't family, that's his cellmate's sidepiece running a hustle with a burner Facebook profile and a stolen selfie. You're not stepping into his world — you're stepping into a pyramid scheme with commissary as the currency. You want a family reunion? Wait till you meet the other five women he's running the same scam on. Bring potato salad, because y'all are funding the same motherfucker together.

From Girlfriend to Inventory Supplier

Here's where it gets nasty: that sweet poem you poured your heart into? Read aloud like slam poetry on the tier. That private lingerie pic you thought was for his eyes only? Passed around faster than a deck of cards in a poker game.

You thought you were feeding him love, but you were just stocking shelves in the prison Walmart. Oreos, hoodies, letters, selfies — everything you send is flipped for profit. You're not his girlfriend, you're the supply chain. And if you're still dumb enough to believe your picture's safe, don't cry when you find out it's paying somebody else's rent on the outside.

The Cold Punchline

So let's wrap this up with the part nobody wants to hear: the "forever" he's selling you is a cheap rental, and you're the one paying utilities. You're not building love, you're financing a scam. Every woman in his rotation thinks she's the exception — the ride-or-die, the soulmate, the miracle. Spoiler: you're all contestants on *Who Wants to Be the Dumbest Bitch Alive?* The prize is debt, heartbreak, and the privilege of being laughed at on the tier.

The only forever in this lie is how long you'll keep bleeding yourself dry before you wake the fuck up.

CHAPTER SIX

Hustler's Tool Box

---

§6.1 – Recognizing the Pattern: Spotting the Script

They All Start Sweet — 'Cause That's How Poison Goes Down

Girl, let's cut the bullshit — these dudes don't start off swinging. Nah, they sugarcoat that poison so it slides down easy. Whether he's doin' two years or dyin' in that bitch, his only weapon is his fuckin' mouth. And trust me, he's sharpened that shit sharper than a shank. He don't got dinners, roses, or respect to give, so he throws words like confetti, hoping one of 'em sticks to your dumb ass heart.

The second you answer that JPay, click that collect call, or hit back on some dusty DM, boom — script time:

- "I knew you was different the second I heard your voice."
- "I can finally breathe when I talk to you."
- "I prayed for a woman like you."

Bitch, please. That ain't love. That's factory-made bullshit. Same cheap-ass lines fired off like bullets, and you ain't the first target. You're just the next one in line.

Mirroring: The Hood Version of Catfishing

Here's the oldest dirty trick in the book — mirroring. He don't actually "get you." He just copies your ass like a bootleg mixtape. You say you're into God? Suddenly he know every Psalm in the Bible. You talk about crystals and moon energy? Now he staring at the moon like he's Erykah Badu's baby daddy. You tell him you lost somebody? He magically "remembers" some tragic story he never mentioned before.

Don't mistake that shit for bonding. It ain't. That's him downloading your life like a fuckin' USB stick, then spitting it back to you dressed up as "we soulmates." Nah, sis. You fell for a mask. Behind that mask? Straight monster.

Recycled Scripts, Fresh Pain

None of this is personal. It's business. His script's been recycled more times than Coke cans. "You my queen." "I can't live without you." "You my last hope." Bitch, he said that shit last week to a whole other chick, and he'll say it again tomorrow. That "breakdown" you thought was real on the phone? Fucking performance art. He don't love you — he managing you. You're not his partner. You're his payroll.

The Emotional Transaction

Every "baby I love you" has a damn price tag. Every "you're all I got" is a fuckin' invoice. He drops just enough crumbs to keep you chasing, but never enough to let you eat. And the second you slow down? Suddenly you ain't loyal, suddenly you the villain, suddenly you "just like everybody else who gave up." That's programming. That's guilt he planted, fear he wired into you, loyalty he engineered.

Bottom line? You don't owe shit to a fuckin' script.

How to Spot the Lies in Real Time

- Love-bombing by week two ain't passion, that's pressure.
- Same sob story on repeat? That's trauma for sale.
- Mama dead one week, alive the next? That's sloppy improv.
- He calls your friends "jealous"? That's him tightening the leash.

Every single move is designed to shut your brain down and jack your emotions up until you can't think straight.

Wake-Up Call: It Ain't Love, It's Business

Quit calling it love. It's a damn transaction. He sells you a dream, you pay in money, time, energy. He stacks his commissary, you stay drained. Real talk —

not every man behind bars is a manipulative piece of shit, but if his words don't match his actions? You ain't talking to a man, baby. You talking to a fuckin' marketer.

He's peddling you a love story in pencil, erasing the ending every time you ask for something real. You deserve more than sweet lies dipped in struggle. You deserve more than being an ATM dressed up as "ride or die." The second you recognize the script? That's when you rip the mask off and save your damn self.

§6.2 – Emotional Detachment

Emotions Ain't Facts — They're Just Reactions

Say this shit out loud, girl: Just 'cause I feel it don't mean it's real. Say it again, louder. That warm fuzzy high when he whispers "baby"? That ain't love, that's your brain squirting out dopamine like a busted soda machine. That chest squeeze when he says "you the only one who understands me"? That ain't divine connection — that's trauma bonding with a bow on it. You ain't in love — you addicted. Addicted to the relief from your own loneliness, abandonment, pain. And guess what? He knows. That's why he keeps dishing little hits like your personal dope man. Don't confuse his bullshit with healing — he feeding off your wounds like a vulture.

Love Bombs & Brain Chemistry

Let's keep it gutter but drag science in: when you get them butterflies 'cause he drops a slick-ass line, that ain't "soulmate energy." That's oxytocin and dopamine — same shit you get from sex, chocolate, or scrolling TikTok at 3 a.m. Now the high is tied to him — his letters, his voice, his approval. He's your plug. Then when he goes quiet? You crash. You scramble, writing more, calling more, sending more. That ain't love, girl — that's fuckin' withdrawal. He don't got magic, he just got timing.

He Ain't Special — He Just Knows the Script

Take the blinders off. He's not deep, he's not woke, he damn sure ain't your blessing. He just knows how to press your weak-ass buttons. He saw your cracks and slid right in. You weren't in love with him, you were in love with being seen. He reflected your fantasies back at you like a dirty mirror and you thought it was fate. Nah, sis — that wasn't fire. That was smoke. You didn't catch a man, you caught a fuckin' hallucination.

The Power of the Pause

Detachment don't mean you cold. It means you stop letting this dude puppeteer your feelings like a clown show. Next time he says, "I miss you," stop. Ask yourself: is that real or just the opening act before he begs for commissary? Learn to hit pause:

- *Don't text back right away.*
- *Reread that letter like it came from a stranger.*
- *Ask: If I wasn't lonely, would this even matter?*

And when your chest tightens like you 'bout to fold? That's the withdrawal, baby. Ride that wave. Let it knock you on your ass if it has to. The peace that comes after? That's your real fix.

Guilt Is a Trap, Not a Compass

He gon' hit you with: "You the only one who's been here." Or "I can't believe you'd leave me now." Girl, that ain't vulnerability, that's emotional extortion. He using guilt like a leash, tugging you back every time you pull away. Fuck that. Say it with me: I don't owe nobody my sanity — especially not some jailhouse manipulator who weaponized my damn heart.

Pull the Plug — No Apology Needed

You don't owe him a speech, a closure talk, or some healing-ass TED Talk about why you leaving. Detachment ain't about his peace, it's about yours. Stop explaining. Stop hoping he changes. Stop leaving the door cracked. He won't. He ain't. And even if by some miracle he does, it ain't your goddamn job to wait around.

What Detachment Really Feels Like

At first? It's ugly. It's burnin'. You'll miss him, you'll reach for the phone, you'll dream up "one last letter." But then? You'll breathe. You'll notice you're not twitching every time the phone rings, not dragging your ass to the mailbox like a fiend. That's freedom, baby. And once you taste that silence? You'll wonder why the fuck you ever chained yourself to his script in the first place.

This Ain't About Being Heartless — It's About Boundaries

Don't let nobody twist it — detachment ain't about turning ice cold. It's about finally giving a fuck about yourself. You got bills, peace, a future. If his presence equals stress, guilt, confusion, and pain? That ain't love, that's a life sentence you signed for free. You're allowed to walk. You're allowed to slam the door. You're allowed to put your crown back on without apologizing.

Final Word: Flip the Fuckin' Switch

Freedom ain't about time. It's about one decision: choosing you. Every. Single. Time. When that needy little voice whispers, "But I love him..." you answer back: "Fuck that. I love me more."

§6.3 – The Exit Strategy: How to Cut Ties Without a Scene

This Ain't a Breakup — It's a Fuckin' Escape Plan

Stop sugarcoating it, sis. You ain't breaking up with some high school boyfriend who forgot Valentine's Day. You're staging a goddamn prison break from a hustler who had you on emotional lockdown like you was serving time with him. This ain't closure, it's survival. He don't need no explanations, no "maybe he'll change," no farewell letter with hearts and tears. That's bait, and if you bite, you right back in the fuckin' cage. You ain't leaving a man — you escaping a handler.

Silence Ain't Weakness — It's a Weapon

The most gangster shit you can do? Go ghost. No "one last call." No "I owe him a goodbye." Bitch, you don't owe him shit. Silence is the loudest *fuck you* you'll ever deliver. Don't text, don't answer, don't peek. When he hits you with the guilt-bombs, let them detonate in his own hands. That silence? That's power, that's freedom, that's you walking away like the boss you should've been from jump.

Step 1: Go Cold or Don't Go At All

Halfway exits are bullshit. You either cut the cord clean, or you still his puppet. Real no-contact looks like this:

- Block every number, burner, and prison line he ever touched.
- Block his "sister," his "homegirl," his fake-ass "cousin." All of 'em.
- Delete every letter, every voicemail, every screenshot. Re-reading that crap is like sipping poison on purpose.
- Lock down your socials. If he can see your life, he still controlling the narrative.
- Hell, change your number if you have to. You don't owe nobody an open door.

This ain't ghosting. This is witness protection for your peace.

Step 2: Shut Down the Loopholes

He's a hustler, baby — he's gonna try to crawl back through side doors. Close 'em before he even knocks.

- *Mutual friends*: Cut 'em or tell 'em to mind their fuckin' business.
- *Fake emergencies*: "I'm in danger, I need you." Bitch, please. He been "in danger" since the day he got locked up.
- *Guilt letters*: Burn them. Don't read 'em, don't reply, don't feed the beast.
- *Third-party check-ins*: "He just wanna know if you're okay." He can eat that curiosity.

Step 3: Rewrite the Routine

This where it gets tough. He wormed his way into your schedule. That 6PM call, those mail runs, the daily drama — that became your ritual. Now? Kill it and replace it.

- Swap call time for gym time.
- Fill your mailbox with Amazon boxes, not jailhouse lies.
- When 6PM rolls around and the phone *don't* ring? Smile, sis. That's freedom dialing.

Step 4: Brace for the Cravings

Let's be real: withdrawal is a bitch. You'll crave the chaos, the voice, the routine. That's not love — that's addiction tryna pull you back. You beat it like this:

- Write the craving out, but never send it.
- Reread the proof — the gaslighting, the lies, the money gone. Don't romanticize your own fuckin' cage.
- Call your real ones — the ones who told you he was trash from day one.
- And if you slip? Don't wallow. Get your ass back up and slam the door harder.

Step 5: Build Your "After Plan"

He ain't gonna take rejection quiet. Some sulk, some escalate. Either way, stay colder than steel.

- New letters? Trash 'em. Don't read a word.
- Messages through other people? Screenshot, block, keep it movin'.
- Show up after release? Call the cops. Fuck that "hear him out" noise.

You don't owe him niceness. You don't owe him shit but absence.

Cutting Ties Is the Real Love Story

Love ain't hanging on until you bleed out. Love is saving your own damn life. You gave him chances, grace, forgiveness. He gave you guilt, lies, and empty-ass promises. The most loving thing you can do now? Give him nothing. Not a dime, not a word, not a tear.

Exit Like a Fuckin' Queen

No last words, no goodbye texts, no "closure." Just silence, distance, and power. Crown straight, chin high. He ain't your man, he ain't your savior. He's a lesson. And you? You finally graduated summa cum laude from Hustler University. Walk the fuck out. And never look back.

§6.4 – Rebuilding Yourself & Regaining Your Independence

First Step: Breathe Without the Fuckin' Leash

That knot in your chest every time the prison number lit your phone? Gone. That little jolt of panic when you saw his sloppy-ass handwriting in the mailbox? Gone. That guilt-trip silence he used to weaponize every time you ain't jump fast enough? Gone, baby. You cut the leash. Now your first job ain't fixing him, proving shit, or explaining yourself. Your first job is breathing. Take a big-ass inhale of that silence. That's *your* air now, not his cage. Let it hit your lungs 'til you finally remember what freedom feels like.

No more walking on eggshells to keep his ass calm.
No more tensing up every time he pulled a mood swing.
No more begging for respect that should've been free from day one.

That chapter? Burn it.

Digging Out the Woman You Buried

Let's keep it real — while you were babysitting his emotions like a full-time job, you lost track of *you*. Where's the woman who used to laugh so hard she snorted? The one who danced in the mirror with no audience? The one who dreamed about more than commissary deposits and phone bills? She's still in there — buried under layers of his bullshit like a diamond in dirt.

Rebuilding means digging that bad bitch back out:

- Do what makes *you* laugh, not what strokes his ego.
- Chase the love you want, not the crumbs you settled for.
- Build a future without his sorry ass chained to your ankle.

This ain't healing — this is a resurrection.

Fixing the Finances He Fucked Up

Let's call it what it is — dude bled your pockets like a vampire. Forty here, five hundred there, phone bills, care packages, "emergencies." He made you feel guilty for even thinking *no*. Time to flip that script.

- Audit the damage. Add it up, not to shame yourself, but so you never forget the cost of his hustle.
- Start a "Rebuild Me" fund. Every dime you used to throw at JPay? Throw it at your damn self. Stack it. Use it for therapy, classes, vacations, tattoos that scream *fuck these lies.*
- Your wallet's closed. Your love life under new management.

Reconnecting With Your Real Ones

Remember the people who warned you? Mama, your bestie, your co-worker who side-eyed you every time you said "he's misunderstood." You probably lied, defended him, maybe even cursed 'em out. But guess what? They still love your messy ass. They'll roast you a little, but they'll ride for you harder than he ever did. Bring them back. Let truth-tellers surround you. Accept love that don't come wrapped in razor wire.

Setting Boundaries With a Fucking Baseball Bat

Old you thought "ride-or-die" meant *die inside* for some man's comfort. Old you thought saying no was selfish. Old you thought love meant struggle. Nah. That version of you is dead.

New rules:

- If it feels manipulative? NO.
- If it drains you? NO.
- If it smells like a recycled script? BYE.
- They call you cold? Say, *"Damn right. Cold keeps my peace alive."*

You didn't crawl outta hell just to land back in another one.

Learning to Trust Your Own Badass Again

Here's the hardest part: forgiving yourself. You probably asked, "How the fuck did I not see it? Am I stupid?" No, baby. You were loyal to the wrong motherfucker, that's all.

Rebuilding trust with yourself means keeping small-ass promises:

- Say you'll walk ten minutes? Do it.
- Say you'll block that number and not peek? Stick to it.
- Say you'll stop answering "hey stranger" texts? Hit delete.

Every little promise you keep proves your gut ain't broken. And when you trust your own damn gut? No con man alive can touch you.

From Survival to Power — The Final Glow-Up

This ain't just healing. This is a glow-up so raw even your old self won't recognize you. You're sharper, louder, harder to play. You ain't scared of being alone. You ain't scared of saying no. And you sure as fuck ain't scared to choose yourself.

Now you know:

- Love without peace is poison.
- "I love you" without action is abuse.
- Your softness is sacred, but your strength? Untouchable.

You survived his hustle. You walked out that cage. Now you walk into your own power like the fuckin' queen you are.

Keisha's Reality Check

Girl, let's keep it 100: this is your rebirth. He stole your time, your money, your peace, your trust — and you still standing. That's hood royalty, baby. Every dollar you save, every boundary you draw, every laugh you reclaim? That's you snatching your crown back from the dirt.

Keisha's Closing Advice

Stay loud about your freedom. Don't whisper it. Don't water it down. And the next slick-mouthed hustler who tries to test you? Remember: you ain't that same chick no more. You ain't a victim — you a survivor turned ruler. Walk like it.

§6.5 Raven Sinclair's Reflections

Cut the Rope or Wear the Noose

Ladies, here's the hard truth: every second you hesitate is another second with the rope tightening around your neck. These hustlers don't leave you breathing room — they train you to think their chaos is your oxygen. But ask yourself: are you breathing freely, or choking quietly? You can't rebuild while you're still tethered to the wreckage. Cut the rope. Stop asking if you're being "too cold." Cold is survival.

Detachment Isn't Cruelty — It's Self-Preservation

Too many women confuse walking away with being heartless. Let me be clear: saving yourself isn't cruel, it's the only intelligent move. Love that drains you, silences you, manipulates you — that isn't love, that's a prison without walls. The longer you justify staying, the deeper you sink into debt — emotional, financial, spiritual. Stop paying a bill that will never be marked "paid in full."

The Blueprint Forward

Here's your formula:

1. **Silence him.** No calls, no letters, no "one last" anything. That's not closure — that's relapse.
2. **Rebuild you.** Replace every dollar wasted with one invested in your future. Replace every routine tied to him with one tied to your growth. Replace guilt with pride — pride in finally choosing yourself.
3. **Trust your instincts again.** You weren't broken, you were conned. Learn the difference.

Your Crown, Your Responsibility

No one's going to hand you respect, peace, or independence — you take it. You build it. You protect it like it's sacred, because it is. Boundaries aren't walls, they're guardrails. They don't keep love out; they keep parasites from crawling in.

Remember this: you are not disposable, and you damn sure are not a man's business plan. You are your own. The moment you stop funding his hustle is the moment you start funding your freedom. Don't hesitate. Don't explain. Don't negotiate. Just move.

Walk out with your head high, crown straight, and understand — the only forever worth chasing is the one where you belong entirely to yourself.

§6.6 Larry Levine's Reflections

The Punchline of the Hustle

Here's the thing nobody wants to say out loud: you weren't in love, you were in business — his business. Chapter 6 spells it out plain. This shit isn't romance, it's an accounting department run out of a cellblock. He's selling dreams wholesale, and you're the sucker buying retail. You weren't "the one." You were a walking ATM with tits, programmed to spit out cash and validation whenever he pressed the right button. And while you were imagining wedding dresses and new beginnings, he was perfecting his script like a shitty actor who's been bombing auditions for twenty years straight.

The Script Ain't Shakespeare, It's Customer Service

You ever notice how every line he feeds you sounds suspiciously polished? "I prayed for you," "you're the only one who understands me," "I knew from the first call you were different." Bitch, please. That's not love, that's the jailhouse equivalent of "Thank you for calling AT&T, how can I fuck your day up?" It's not original, it's not romantic, it's not special. It's a script, recycled harder than old Hustler magazines passed around on the tier. He's not your soulmate. He's a telemarketer in shackles, dialing until someone says yes.

Silence Is the Ultimate "Fuck You"

Let me break it down: if you think you need one last call, one last letter, one last goodbye, you're not leaving — you're negotiating your own relapse. Closure is a scam. You don't need closure with a hustler, you need distance. Silence is nuclear. It's the only move that actually rattles them because they can't play chess without a pawn on the board. When you vanish — cold, clean, no warning — you steal the only currency they ever had: your attention. That's the biggest "fuck you" you'll ever deliver.

Stop Pretending "Healing" Is Pretty

You know what rebuilding looks like? Not yoga classes, not bubble baths, not some Instagram post about "self-love." It looks like sitting in your apartment ugly-crying, realizing you got played, and deciding you're done being a mark. It looks like checking your bank statement, adding up the hundreds you blew on ramen noodles and phone time, and saying, "Never again." It looks like laughing at your own stupidity, not hiding from it. Healing isn't pretty — it's raw, it's loud, it's clawing your crown out of the dirt and putting it back on sideways. And guess what? Sideways still means you're wearing the crown.

Rebuilding Ain't Optional — It's Survival

You don't rebuild for Instagram likes, you rebuild because the alternative is staying a broke, bitter shell of yourself while he moves on to his next victim. Rebuilding means reclaiming every dollar, every boundary, every shred of dignity he stole. It means telling yourself "no more" and backing it up with action. He drained you, lied to you, guilt-tripped you, used you — but the moment you pull the plug, all that power shifts back in your corner. Rebuilding isn't a choice. It's the only way out of the cage.

The Real Glow-Up — Graduation Day

You want to know what the glow-up really looks like? It's the day you stop twitching when the phone rings. The day you laugh at his "I miss you" letters instead of crying into your pillow. The day you finally admit that "I love you" without action is just emotional abuse in lingerie. That's not love, it's poison — and you've been drinking it like Kool-Aid. The real glow-up is walking the fuck away, crown straight, middle finger raised, summa cum laude graduate of Hustler University. You passed the course. Don't you dare retake it.

CHAPTER SEVEN

The Isolation Game

§7.1 – Devon Was the Lesson, Not the Love

He Slid in Like a Fuckin' Roach

Devon didn't "walk" into my life, nah. That man slithered in like a goddamn roach when the lights off. Quiet, slick, dirty. I wasn't even looking for nobody — I had my guard up, heart padlocked tighter than a bank vault. But hustlers? They smell cracks like blood in the water. He found mine.

And he was slick as hell about it. He didn't come begging right out the gate. No, he came soft. He listened. Long-ass phone calls where he soaked up every word, feeding me back that "you're so strong, you're so different" line like it was gospel. He told me I ain't sound like them other women who write. That I was special. A blessing. And stupid-ass me? I believed every word.

He didn't have to ask for shit — he made me offer it.
"Baby, I hate asking you this…"
"You know I'd never use you, right?"
"If I had another way, I wouldn't even bring it up…"

That's how the game runs. Gentle manipulation wrapped in fake-ass vulnerability. It wasn't love. It was a con dressed up in Hallmark bullshit. And me? I was the audience clapping while he picked my pockets.

He Built Me Up Just to Drain Me Dry

It started with time, not money. He had me scheduling my life around his goddamn prison calls. Leaving work early. Missing family dinners. Sitting hunched over Dollar Tree stationery pouring my heart out like he was Shakespeare. Time was the down payment.

Then came the upsell. Commissary. "Cellie's stealing from me." "I'm sick." "I need meds." Every sob story had a dollar sign glued to it. And every dollar I sent bought me another spoonful of affection.

And when I hesitated? He flipped the script. Not rage — oh no, Devon was slicker than that. He used disappointment. Silence. Guilt. Made me feel like I was the bad guy, like I was abandoning him in his darkest hour. I wasn't helping my man, I was keeping his hustle alive.

The Fantasy Was the Real Drug

I wasn't hooked on Devon — I was hooked on the *idea* of Devon. The porch, the Sunday dinners, him holding my back in the grocery store. I fed that fantasy like it was my full-time job, and it damn near killed me.

Every time I tried to step back, he reeled me in with that half-ass accountability:
"I know I've been selfish, but I'm trying, baby."
"You're my anchor. My reason. I swear I'll make it right."

Man could sell a dream better than any televangelist rocking a Rolex. And I kept tithing, thinking one day the "blessing" would show up. Spoiler alert: it never did.

When the Mask Cracked, So Did My Patience

Devon got sloppy. Lies leaked like a busted toilet. Said one thing in a call, another in a letter. Called me by the wrong nickname. Got defensive when I asked simple-ass questions. It wasn't some big exposé, but it was enough. Enough for that little voice in my head — the one I kept drowning in his bullshit — to scream: *"This ain't love, sis. This a goddamn job, and you're the only one clocking in."*

I didn't argue. Didn't demand an explanation. I already knew what I'd get: another excuse, another guilt trip, another fresh coat of paint on the same old lie. So I did what I hadn't tried yet. I went cold.

Blocked his number. Stopped writing. Slammed the fuckin' door.

Leaving Didn't Break Me — Staying Did

That first week? Hell. Phantom phone buzzes. Mailbox twitches. I cried — not for him, but for the version of me that used to feel strong before his ass drained me dry.

But then the silence hit different. Sacred. I didn't flinch when the phone rang. Didn't feel guilty for buying myself shit. Slept through the night without dreams of prison walls and his needy-ass voice.

I wasn't just healing. I was coming back to life.

Rebuilding Me Was the Real Flex

I stopped hiding what happened. I told other women. I wrote about it. I warned them. I stacked my money. Fixed my credit. Started the business I'd been talking about forever. Went to therapy — not for him, but for me. To kill that version of myself that thought I had to play savior just to feel worth loving.

Devon schooled me. He showed me manipulation don't always sound like rage — sometimes it sounds like "I love you." He showed me how words without proof are cheap as hell. But most of all, he showed me my own fucking power once I stopped pouring it into a grown man who refused to grow.

To Every Woman Reading This: Wake the Fuck Up

If you're in it right now — still answering calls, still sending packages, still swallowing that pit in your stomach every time he says, "This is the last time, baby" — let me hit you with truth:

You're not stupid. You're not weak. You're not worthless.
 You're just believing in somebody who ain't earned an ounce of that belief.

But you can stop. You can walk. And when you do? That silence you're scared of? That shit will turn into freedom. The kind you can breathe. The kind you can live in. The kind you'll never trade again.

CHAPTER EIGHT

Why Real Love is Rare

§8.1 – Guardrails Against the Hustle

Don't Get It Twisted — Real Love in This Game Is Scarce as Hell

Girl, let's keep it a hunnid: real love behind them bars? Rare as fuck. Rarer than a CO lettin' you sneak a burner through intake. It *can* happen — I ain't sayin' it don't — but you got a better shot at hittin' Powerball back-to-back while yo' deadbeat baby daddy magically pays child support on time.

These dudes ain't thinkin' about your forever. They sittin' on concrete beds with too much time, cheap-ass pens, and buckets of desperation. Time + hunger = hustler. Period. They not writin' you 'cause they plannin' the white-picket-fence dream. They writin' you 'cause somebody gotta keep them soups stacked and their fragile-ass ego stroked.

And if you sittin' at home lonely, vulnerable, or just need a lil' "you special, baby" talk? Boom — you target practice.

The play always starts sweet:

- "Baby, I prayed for a woman like you."
- "You the only one who gets me."
- "Damn, I can't believe you even wrote me."

Sound familiar? Don't play dumb. We've all heard it. And yeah, it hits 'cause you wanna believe it. But let me slap some reality in you:

That shit ain't personal. It's professional. He been rehearsin' them lines like mixtape drops. You ain't special, girl. You just the one on the call rotation tonight.

Love Ain't Supposed to Feel Like a Hustle

Here's some real Atlanta game for you: love ain't supposed to feel like homework you didn't sign up for. It ain't supposed to feel like Six Flags with no seatbelt. If it's up one day, ghosted the next? That ain't passion, that's manipulation with a condom on.

Love is steady. Consistent. If he flippin' the script every week — one day it's "you my queen," next day he ghost like Casper? Sis, he not lovin' you, he *training* you to chase.

- Real love respects "no." If he wildin' every time you don't send him $100? That's not a man, that's a beggar with bars.
- Real love don't fuck with your head. If you doubting yourself every other day over his bullshit? That ain't Cupid — that's a scammer with a pen pal.

The Game They're Really Playin'

Don't get it twisted — they ain't buildin' love, they buildin' a fuckin' pyramid scheme. They pull women in like recruits, gas you up as the "main," then sit back while commissary deposits rain in from all sides.

One of the dirtiest plays? The "one percent" line. "Baby, you my one percent. You different." Yeah, and the chick in Ohio and the one in Dallas just got the same script copy-pasted. You not his one percent — you his percentage point.

Every "I love you" got a price tag. Every "you all I got" is just a way to make sure you don't check the receipts.

How to Tell If It's Real — Or Just a Dirty Script

Here's the hood checklist, no sugarcoat:

- **Consistency** – Writes love letters but forgets your birthday? Hustle.
- **Boundaries** – Every convo ends in "send money"? Hustle.
- **Receipts** – Stories don't match week-to-week? Hustle.
- **Energy** – You givin' 100, he givin' 25? Hustle.
- **Isolation** – Tryna cut off yo' friends and mama? Hustle.

Now flip it. Real might look like:

- He don't rush you with "forever" bullshit.
- He respects "no" without actin' like a lil' bitch.
- His actions actually match his mouth.
- He got plans for his own damn future.

Anything less? Sis, you already know what time it is.

The Trap of "Feelin' Special"

This the Achilles heel. He make you feel "chosen." Like he passed up the whole damn free world just for you. Reality check: being chosen ain't shit when he picked five more.

That soulmate line? He been photocopyin' that scam since his first county bid. Loneliness is his fertilizer, and you the crop.

- Real love don't make you ignore your gut.
- Real love don't make you cry more than you laugh.
- Real love don't leave you at 3AM wonderin' why he ain't called.

Guardrails to Save Yo' Sanity

Even if you think it's solid, you better strap on some armor. Guardrails, survival fences, call 'em what you want:

- Never let him be your only source of validation.
- Keep yo' bank account *separate*. Love don't need no damn deposit slip.
- Protect yo' circle. Don't ditch mama and your girls for a dude you can't even touch.
- Demand proof. Family, paperwork, consistency — no receipts, no buy-in.

Guardrails don't block love. They block lies.

Keisha's Real Talk Wrap-Up

Look, girl, I know you wanna believe. But nine times outta ten, you ain't fallin' in love — you fallin' in line with a con.

- Don't chase the fantasy, chase reality.

- Don't settle for recycled scripts, demand receipts.
- Don't confuse bein' used with bein' loved.

If he ain't consistent, if he ain't respectin' you, if his words don't match his grind? He ain't yo' forever — he's your *fuckin' liability*.

The faster you clock the hustle, the faster you stop bein' the mark. In this game? Real love don't need a hustle. And hustlers don't deserve your love.

§8.2 – Signs of the Real Thing: Consistency and Boundaries

Consistency Ain't Optional — It's the Whole Damn Test

Listen, sis — real love ain't moody like a broke-ass prepaid phone. It don't flip-flop like MetroPCS service in the hood. If he tellin' you "you my forever" on Monday, then actin' like you don't exist on Thursday? That ain't love, that's a motherfuckin' hustle gift-wrapped in a Hallmark card.

Real love shows up steady. Every. Damn. Day.

- If he callin' only when commissary due? Hustle.
- If he disappear every time you press him with questions? Hustle.
- If you carryin' the whole damn load while he "findin' hisself"? Hustle.

Consistency is the goddamn receipt. And if he ain't got receipts? He ain't got love.

Boundaries Ain't Suggestions, They Survival

Girl, stop lettin' these jailhouse Romeos bulldoze your peace 'cause you think loyalty means sayin' yes to every fuckin' thing. Fuck that. Boundaries keep you from turnin' into his personal ATM and late-night therapy hotline rolled into one.

Real love gon' respect your "no" without throwin' a tantrum like a toddler at Walmart. Real love don't hit you with guilt trips like, "If you really loved me, you would…" That's emotional extortion, not affection.

Check the bullshit meter:

- If he call you selfish 'cause you keep somethin' for yourself? He ain't it.
- If choosin' peace over his drama gets labeled betrayal? He ain't it.

- If he only show love when you bend over backwards? Baby, he ain't lovin' you — he runnin' game on you.

Shared Goals or Shared Fantasy?

Let's keep it all the way Atlanta real: dreams without action? Straight-up lies. If all he talkin' about is "when I get out we gon' buy a house, a Benz, two pit bulls, and open a business," but right now he can't even keep his commissary straight? That ain't vision, that's *bedtime stories for grown-ass women.*

Real love means y'all movin' in the same damn direction. Even locked up, he should be on his grind — takin' classes, cleanin' up, makin' plans that ain't just words. If the only thing he's buildin' is excuses, sis, you just payin' rent in his fantasy.

Ask yourself:

- Are y'all actually liftin' each other up or just draggin' his dead weight?
- Is he makin' moves to be a better man, or just sellin' you "one day" bullshit?
- Do you got actual steps together, or just pillow talk scribbled on JPay?

If he ain't walkin' it, don't you dare keep talkin' it.

The Cold Truth: Match Energy or GTFO

You can't clap with one hand. You can't build a house alone while he sittin' on his ass collectin' your grind like rent. If he ain't matchin' your energy, your love, your respect — he ain't your man, he's your drain.

And the longer you chase his half-ass, the deeper you sink. Love ain't supposed to feel like homework. Love ain't supposed to feel like you beggin' for shit you already deserve.

If he ain't on your level, girl, stop stoopin'. Walk the fuck away before he eats another year of your life.

Keisha's Real Talk

Stop lettin' these clowns convince you your worth is tied to how much you give. Fuck that. If he ain't consistent, if he don't respect your "no," if he ain't buildin' shit but excuses — that ain't love, that's a hustle with lipstick on.

And don't you forget — **you ain't no damn mark.** You're not a stepping stone, you're the whole fuckin' road. If he don't rise to meet you? Tell that motherfucker to kick rocks. You deserve a partner, not a parasite.

§8.3 – Testing the Waters: Make Sure Words Match Actions

Talk Is Cheap — Show Me the Fuckin' Receipts.

Girl, lemme break it down plain: *anybody* can say "I love you." That shit don't cost a dime. Anybody can promise you a house, two kids, a dog, and a happily-ever-after. Hell, he can paint you a whole-ass Disney movie from his bunk. But if there ain't no action behind that script? That shit worth less than Monopoly money. Cute to look at, can't buy you shit.

Stop gettin' hypnotized by pillow talk. Start watchin' the *patterns*. Does he *move* when he says he gon' move? Or do you end up doin' all the damn heavy liftin' while he keep feedin' you "one day" bullshit?

Real love ain't lip service. It's *labor*. If he stuck on repeat like a bootleg mixtape — same "someday, baby" lies every week? That ain't love, sis, that's theater. And you payin' front-row ticket prices every fuckin' time.

The Real Test: Time, Consistency, and Follow-Through

Here's the formula, no sugarcoat: **time + consistency = truth.**

- If he only gets sweet when commissary due? Hustle.
- If he pop up lovey-dovey only when he lonely? Hustle.
- If he ghost for three days then slide back with "I miss you"? Hustle.

Real men don't just *talk* it — they *walk* that shit daily. They respect your time, keep their word, and show the fuck up. If you find yourself doin' all the chasing — callin', writin', beggin', explainin' — you not in a relationship. You in a one-woman play where you the cast, crew, and audience. That ain't love, that's free labor.

The "Time-Test" — Don't Rot in Limbo

Stop lettin' these dudes sell you the "just wait for me" scam. How long you gon' keep yo' life on pause while he "figures shit out"? A real one don't need five years to decide if you the one. He show you *now*. Not "after release." Not "when I get on my feet." Not "one day."

If you holdin' down the fort while he out here stallin'? Baby, that ain't a partnership. That's purgatory with a JPay login. Quit wastin' seasons of your life waitin' on a man who don't even own a fuckin' clock.

Spot the Cycle — And Break That Bitch

The scam runs on repeat, and it looks like this:

1. He love-bombs you. Sweet talk, future talk, "queen this, soulmate that."
2. Shit gets real — you ask for clarity.
3. *Poof.* He gone. Two, three, five days. Silence.
4. He slither back with, "I miss you, baby," or "been thinkin' about you nonstop."
5. You let him back in. Boom. Cycle reset.

Sis, if you can already see this loop playin' out? You already know the answer. That ain't love. That's control. He got you on standby like a Lyft ride while he decides if you worth the effort. Spoiler alert: if he really thought you were, you wouldn't be guessin'.

Keisha's Real Talk — Actions Over Echoes

Fuck the pretty words. If his moves don't line up with his mouth, that shit's trash. Love ain't about poems, promises, or pillow talk — it's about *consistency*. If he ain't showin' up, if he ain't matchin' your energy, if he's draggin' you through the same cycle till you drained and broke? Baby, walk the fuck away. No explanations. No warnings. No second chances.

You don't need a poet. You don't need a dream-seller. You need a man whose *actions* say what his lips can't fake. **You deserve action, not auditions.**

§8.4 – Guardrails: Protectin' Yourself Even If It's Real

Don't Get Caught Slippin'

Girl, lemme put you on some *real hood game*: even if you manage to find one of the unicorn-ass dudes who might actually mean it, you still can't fold all the way. Don't go actin' like you hit the love lottery and drop your guard. Love don't erase the fact you been played, drained, and lied to before. Matter fact, love just makes you a *bigger* target, 'cause once you feel safe? That's when you get sloppy. And in this game, sloppy = food.

And don't get it twisted — you ain't just guardin' against him. You guardin' against *you*. Against the part of you that wanna believe so bad you ignore the red flags, confuse attention with affection, and think struggle equals loyalty. That soft-ass part of you is dangerous as fuck.

Respect My Fuckin' Boundaries

Here's the real test, no Hallmark, no sugar:

- If I say *no* and you keep pressin'? That ain't passion — that's predatory.
- If you guilt trip me with "If you really loved me, you would..."? That's emotional extortion, not love.
- If every line I draw you try to push back? That ain't compromise, that's control.

Real love don't demand you kill parts of yourself just to prove loyalty. Real love stands inside your boundaries with you, not try to bulldoze 'em down.

Guardrails Ain't Weakness, They Fuckin' Armor

Some of y'all got brainwashed into thinkin' boundaries make you "cold," "bitter," or "unreachable." Nah, that's bullshit. Boundaries don't mean you broken — they mean you *trained*. You learned the hard way that when you hand somebody the keys to your peace, nine times outta ten they drive that bitch straight into a ditch.

Guardrails ain't blockin' love — they filterin' out bullshit. They the line between a man who respects you and a man who just tryna *drain* you.

So repeat after me:

- If it feels manipulative? It's a no.
- If it leaves me empty? It's a no.
- If it sound rehearsed like he practiced it in the mirror? It's a no.

Love Ain't Gon' Save You From Your Own Dumb Choices

Real shit: you could love somebody with every drop of your heart, but that won't stop you from gettin' played if you don't love yourself enough to set standards.

Love ain't no bulletproof vest. It don't pay bills, it don't heal trauma, and it sure as hell don't erase you ignorin' your gut.

Stop tellin' yourself "But he loves me" like it's a damn get-out-of-jail-free card. If you don't protect yourself, nobody else will. That's the number one rule in this game.

Validate Yo'self First, Always

Half the reason women get caught up is 'cause they hungry for validation. They waitin' on a man to say "you beautiful, you worthy, you enough.

" But baby, you *already enough*. A real man gon' add to that. A hustler gon' exploit the fact you don't believe it yet.

So stop handin' out your worth like EBT cards to every smooth-tongued con in khakis. If he really love you, he gon' multiply what you already know. If he makin' you doubt it? That ain't love — that's fuckin' theft.

Keisha's Real Talk – Boundaries = Fuckin' Power

Don't confuse "ride-or-die" with "ride-or-stupid." If he call you selfish for sayin' no, cold for protectin' your peace, or heartless for not lettin' him run game? Flip it back:

"Nah, I ain't cold. I just stopped lettin' clowns run the circus in my heart."

Guardrails ain't optional. They ain't "maybe." They the *blueprint* for survival. Real love gon' honor 'em. Fake love gon' test 'em. And your job? Enforce 'em every time, no flinchin'.

So even if it feel real, even if he seem solid, keep them walls high. 'Cause the second you start slippin'? That's the second you back in the same bullshit cycle. And girl — we not doin' re-runs no more.

§8.5 Devon's Fantasy: How I Got Played and Walked Away

Now lemme drop a personal receipt. Devon — yeah, that motherfucker — he was the perfect case study in how these locked-up clowns run game. He slid in smooth as hell, all charm and "baby, you different." Talkin' like he was heaven-sent, droppin' lines right where I was soft.

And me? I was vulnerable, fresh off some bullshit. So I bit. He had me imaginin' houses, babies, family BBQs — the whole hood-picket-fence fantasy. But every promise was just a leash.

The guilt game was his favorite: "If it wasn't for you, I don't know how I'd survive in here." Translation? *Bitch, keep sendin' the money.* And dumbass me? I did. Pictures, letters, JPay, packages — I was his personal ATM with a side of therapy.

Then came the slip. He vanish for days. No calls. No letters. I'm stressin', thinkin' maybe somethin' happened. He finally pop up like, "Baby, I was just busy, but you know you all I think about." Busy? Busy doin' *what*, motherfucker? You locked up! But I let it slide 'cause by then I was hooked on the fantasy.

But lies don't stay buried. One day I catch his phone blowin' up with another chick's name. Same lines, same pics, same damn hustle. He was servin' me reheated bullshit he was feedin' her too.

That's when it cracked. He wasn't different. He wasn't special. He was a *copy-paste con.*

And yeah, I was hurt. Embarrassed. Felt dumb as hell. But here's the twist: that shit made me sharper. I cut him off — no goodbye, no closure, just block, delete, fuck you very much.

Did I miss him? Hell no. I missed the routine, the attention, the *lie.* But once I saw it for what it was, I couldn't unsee it.

Now Devon? He just a fuckin' cautionary tale I feed to other women. He thought he played me. Nah — I graduated. And now I use his bullshit like a textbook. Lesson learned: if the words don't match the actions, walk. No explanations. No second chances.

§8.6 Raven's Commentary on Chapter Eight

The Scarcity of Real Love

Keisha's right — real love in this game is damn near extinct. But let's go deeper: it's not just because men inside are hustling, it's because the *entire environment* is engineered to breed manipulation. Prison is starvation mode. Starvation of power, intimacy, control, identity. Men in cages turn to the only weapons they have: words. They sharpen "I love you" the way another man sharpens a shank. If you don't understand that, you're not just naïve — you're chum in the water.

The Psychological Hook

Every woman who falls thinks she's immune until she isn't. Loneliness is the lever, fantasy is the fulcrum, and desperation is the weight. Once you believe you're "the exception," you're already compromised. That's the psychology of a hustle: convince you you're special while proving you're disposable. It's not love — it's a system of emotional extraction.

The Currency of Lies

Here's the truth most won't admit: the man isn't the product — *you are*. Your attention, your money, your loyalty. That's the commodity. His "love" is just the currency he spends to get it. Every letter, every phone call, every half-ass promise is an investment in keeping you tethered. If you can't see that, you're the asset on his balance sheet.

The Brutality of Guardrails

Keisha calls them guardrails, and she's right — but I'll sharpen it. Boundaries aren't just defense, they're weapons. Every "no" is a cut. Every refusal to be guilt-tripped is a strike. If you don't swing those weapons, don't act surprised when you end up gutted. Women think boundaries make them hard. No — boundaries keep you from being butchered. That's not cruelty. That's survival.

The Lesson of Devon

Her story about Devon? Multiply that by ten thousand and you've got the national average. The names change. The details shift. The mechanics stay identical. What she lived wasn't unique — it was the template. The only difference between the women who walk away and the ones who get buried in it is whether they believe their own worth more than they believe his lies.

Final Cut

If you take anything from this chapter, take this:

- If his words are bigger than his actions, it's a hustle.

- If your love costs you more than it gives back, it's a hustle.
- If you're doubting your value more than you're feeling loved, it's a hustle.

You don't owe him your loyalty. You owe yourself your life.

§8.7 Larry Levine Commentary

You want the ugly truth? Love in prison is like a unicorn smoking crack — people *swear* it exists, but you ain't never seen one outside of some fairy tale bullshit. Everybody wants to believe they're "the exception." You're not. You're just the next name on the rotation.

Let me spell it out: these motherfuckers got nothin' but time, and they're weaponizing it against you. Prison hustlers write "I love you" the way car salesmen say "low mileage." It's a pitch. You ain't their soulmate — you're their customer. The product? Your wallet. The packaging? Some sweet talk wrapped in "forever" promises they've recycled on half a dozen other suckers this week.

But nah, you wanna believe. Because it feels good. Because it scratches that itch of being "special." Spoiler: if he's telling you you're "different," you're not. He's running the same script he's been perfecting since county lockup. You're just dumb enough to clap for it this round.

Here's a reality check:

- Real love doesn't come with a payment plan.
- Real love doesn't ghost you when commissary's full and reappear the second it's empty.
- Real love doesn't guilt-trip you into wiring cash while he's "finding himself." Newsflash — he's not finding shit. He's found a victim. You.

And guardrails? They ain't some cute metaphor — they're survival. If you don't enforce boundaries, you're not "loyal," you're livestock. Stop crying about why he don't respect you while you keep playing doormat with open pockets. You trained him to bleed you dry, so congratulations — you're now the unofficial Warden of Dumbass Decisions.

Devon's story? Please. That's not some dramatic, one-in-a-million betrayal. That's the fucking *default setting*. You didn't find a hustler in the haystack, you found the haystack. The only thing shocking is that you thought it was love. That's like mistaking a pickpocket for a dance partner just because he smiled at you while stealing your shit.

So here's my big Levine wrap-up: if you're sitting at 3 a.m. staring at your phone wondering why he hasn't called, let me save you the suspense — it's because you're not the only one. You're just one of the ones. If that stings, good. Maybe it'll slap you awake before you waste another year of your life being a side character in his little prison soap opera.

Stop falling for scripts. Stop paying for fairy tales. And for fuck's sake — stop confusing being used with being loved.

The Family & Legal Trap

What These Modules Cover

Module 3 is where the hustle graduates. By now, the sweet talk's run its course — it's about money, leverage, and dragging you deeper into his world. The game shifts from romance to strategy, and you're not just a girlfriend anymore. You're the ATM, the secretary, the paralegal, and sometimes the fool at the front of the line cosigning his bullshit.

CHAPTER 9 – Family Ties That Choke

When Mama calls you "baby," it ain't love — it's recruitment. His whole family knows the script, and you're not the queen of the castle, you're the newest investor. Every "he's a good man" pep talk is just a pitch to keep your money flowing and your doubts on mute. You're not joining a family. You're buying into a syndicate.

CHAPTER 10 – Legal Hustles

This is where the scam puts on a suit. Lawyers that don't exist. Paralegals named "cousin Tasha." Power of attorney tricks that turn your name into his cash pipeline. You're told you're "helping with the appeal," but really? You're financing commissary, fake filings, and his ego. The law ain't his redemption — it's his new hustle, and you're footing the bill.

The Real Takeaway

Module 3 shows you the scam ain't just a one-man show — it's a fucking ensemble cast. Mama, cousins, fake lawyers, and even notarized paperwork all play their part in bleeding you dry. And if you ain't careful? You won't just lose your heart, you'll lose your credit score, your savings, and your sanity.

This ain't about love anymore — this is logistics. And if you don't cut the cord now, you're gonna find yourself broke, bitter, and legally tied to a man who's never coming home.

CHAPTER NINE

The Family Hustle

§9.1 Family Scams and How His People Hustle You

The Game Ain't Just Him — It's the Whole Damn Family

Listen up, girl, I'm about to hit you with some cold truth. This ain't just about him—it's about the whole damn family, and you're just another part of the game they're running. You think it's just your man? Nah, he's the front. But behind him, there's an entire operation. His mama, his sisters, his cousins—they're all working their angles, keeping you emotionally tied up while they play you for everything you're worth.

Mama — The Sweet Face of the First Hustle

It starts slow. Mama comes in first, right? She's the one making you feel like you're the only one who understands him. She'll call you, text you, talk all nice, tell you how much she appreciates you for being there for her son. She'll throw in some stories about how hard he's had it, how he's a good man deep down, and how he just needs a chance. You're thinking, "Damn, maybe I'm the one who can hold him down." You feel like you're doing the right thing, right? Sending a little bit of money here, maybe a couple packages there, keeping him feeling good while he's locked up.

But here's the twist: mama isn't just some sweet woman who cares about you—she's the first line in the hustle. She's out here playing on your emotions, using that guilt to make you send more. "He needs you, girl. You're the only one who can keep him strong. Just a little more support, and he'll get through this." And before you know it, you've sent cash, snacks, and those cute little pics. But that's not just for him—it's part of a bigger picture. She's making sure you stay tied into this long-term game, keeping you emotionally invested so you'll keep giving.

Sisters & The Fake "Family" Circle

Then comes the sisters—they get in the mix, too. They'll be all sweet, talking about how much they appreciate you being there for their brother. They'll send you the "I'm family" vibe, acting like they're just looking out for you, but it's all a ploy. They know exactly what they're doing—making you feel like you're part of the circle, part of the inner family. They'll pull that "I'm his sister, and we've got your back, too" card. It's all about getting you to think that you're helping the whole family, not just him. It's a psychological game to make you feel like you're part of something bigger, like you belong, so you'll keep sending.

The Dirty Secret — You're Just a Source

But here's the dirty little secret: they don't care about you. They care about what you're sending. They care about your loyalty to the game. As long as you're sending money and gifts, as long as you're emotionally invested, you're just another source of income. That "I miss you, baby"?

That's not love—that's the family working together to make sure you keep giving. They'll make sure you stay emotionally tied to him, making you think he's the one who needs you, that he's your soulmate. But the reality is, he's using that to get what he wants while the rest of the family is eating off you, too.

Now, you're thinking it's just you and him. You think you're the one he's really after. But while you're out there thinking you're his ride or die, they're all working the angle. Mama's making sure you stay hooked. Sister's hitting you up to keep the money flowing. Cousins and homeboys are out there putting pressure on you, too, acting like they're your friends, asking for help with their own "problems." It's a team hustle, and you're the mark.

The thing is, they know exactly how to play you. They've been doing it for years—using guilt, using empathy, making you think that if you just keep supporting him, it's all gonna work out. They'll play on your loyalty, making you feel like you're the only one holding him down while everyone else is too selfish to help. They know that once they've got you emotionally attached, you'll keep giving. And once you start giving, they know you're hooked.

Keisha's Real Talk — Wake the Hell Up

Girl, it's time to wake up and see what's going on. You ain't just dealing with him—you're dealing with a whole operation that's been working you over from the start. You think it's just him needing you, but it's his whole family, and they're all in on the hustle. Mama, sister, cousin, they're all part of the game. You're the source, and they're making sure you keep feeding it. Recognize the game before you lose yourself in it. They're not about love, they're about what you can give

§9.2 Sending Love – Gifts and Phone Call Tactics

Love or Currency?

You think the gifts are love? Nah, baby girl, they're tactics. Straight up. Every time you send him a care package, every time you're out here buying him snacks, clothes, and whatever else he wants, guess what? You ain't sending love, you're sending currency. And that phone call you get where he's all sweet, talking 'bout how he's thinking of you, how he's missing you? It's not love, it's a play.

The Phone Call Control Game

Let me break it down. The phone calls? They're not just for him to hear your voice. They're a tool—a way for him to control the situation, keep you emotionally invested. Every time he calls you, he's not just calling to say "I miss you"—he's calling to reinforce the control. He's pulling you back in, making you feel like you're needed, and in return, you're giving him more: money, attention, stuff.

When Gifts Become Hustle

When you're out there buying him clothes, sending those "thinking of you" packages, or those lingerie pics, guess what? He's selling them to his boys. The clothes? Resold. The pictures? Passed around like they're part of his side hustle. You're sitting there thinking you're helping him get by, but really? You're part of his emotional economy, and everything you send has a price tag attached to it. It's a hustle.

He'll play you with those sweet words, but every time you pick up that phone, you're getting reel in deeper. When he says things like, "Baby, I need you, you're all I got out here," you're not just helping him feel loved. You're making him feel secure—and that makes it easier for him to get what he needs: attention, money, and support. And while you're over there thinking you're just being the loving girl, he's sitting pretty, knowing you're locked in, hooked by his words.

The Pattern You Don't See

Here's the kicker: it's all a pattern. He knows exactly when to call you, exactly when to drop that "I miss you" line, and he knows exactly when to turn on the charm when you start pulling away. It's the same tactic every time. You start getting distance? He's calling, saying things like, "I need you right now. You don't know how hard this is." You get those sweet promises, talking about how things will be different when he gets out, how you're the one who's gonna hold him down. But it's just another play to make sure you keep feeding the game.

You think the phone calls are a moment of connection? Nah, they're just to keep you emotionally tied. They're designed to keep you in the game, getting you to send more money, more care packages, and more emotional energy. Meanwhile, his boys are out there using your stuff to feed their hustle too, passing around pictures, flip-selling things you sent, and making sure everyone eats while you keep giving.

Keisha's Real Talk — Don't Confuse It for Love

You gotta stop thinking this is love. These phone calls? The gifts? The "I miss you" lines? They're part of a game. A game where you're the mark. If you keep sending him stuff, you're not helping him make it through, you're helping him keep his life comfortable while you keep getting played. Real love don't make you chase. It don't make you feel used. It's time to check the hustle, girl, and realize that you're worth more than being just another part of his game. Don't fall for it.

§9.3 The Visit Room Illusion

The Stage, Not the Love

You think those visits are the real deal, right? You're thinking this is the time, the moment where love connects. But girl, that visit room is just another stage in the hustle. The whole thing? It's illusion. All that sweet talk about how he's counting the days until you can be together? That's just part of the hustle to make sure you keep coming back, keep giving him money, emotional energy, and everything he needs to feel like he's in control.

What He's Really Thinking When You Walk In

He's not just thinking about the romance, he's thinking about what you're bringing with you when you walk in. Is it a care package? Is it extra cash for his commissary? Is it more attention that he can sell to the next woman? Girl, those visits are a chance for him to check in, assess how hooked you are, and make sure you're still down to keep feeding the hustle.

You think that smile when he sees you is for you? Nah, it's for what you can give. It's all part of the play. He's already running through his head what he can get out of you, what he can ask for next. When you're sitting there, talking about the future, you think it's about the two of you building something. No, it's about him setting you up for the next ask—asking you to send money for his legal fees, or make a deposit for his phone, or just send more money because "he's starving" and "needs to get by."

The Business Transaction Masked as Love

And the visit itself? It's not some romantic reunion where you get to spend the day loving on each other, building a future. It's a business transaction, where he makes sure you're still invested, still emotionally tied, still feeding the game. When you leave, he knows he's got you—you've given him attention, maybe a little more money, and you're back out in the world, thinking about how romantic that visit felt. But that visit wasn't about love—it was about keeping you locked into the game.

You go in there thinking this is a real connection—you're touching his hand, you're making eye contact, you're talking about the life you're gonna have when he gets out. But that's the illusion—because when the visit's over, you're back to the grind, back to him asking for more. And you're thinking you're just being supportive, but he's keeping you in the cycle—the one where you give more and more, while he sits back and plays his part, making you feel like you're the only one.

The Reality of It All – It's Not About You, It's About the Hustle

Girl, when you leave those visits, you've gotta realize something—it wasn't about you, and it wasn't about him loving you. It was about him getting what he needs, using his charm and your emotions to make sure you're still coming back to the game. He's gonna hit you with that guilt, with those "I miss you so much, I can't wait for you to be with me" lines. And you're gonna be sitting there thinking it's real. But when you look back, you're gonna realize—he ain't thinking about the future, he's thinking about what you can give him.

You think your visit meant something? Nah. It was a part of the game, a way to keep you locked in emotionally. He's gonna hit you with that soft talk, but don't get caught up. The reality is, he's out here trying to get as much as he can from you without giving a damn about your needs. He's playing on your emotions, pulling you in, making you feel like he's your soulmate, while he's working his angles behind the scenes.

Keisha's Real Talk – Don't Let Him Keep You Hooked

Girl, don't let these visits fool you. **Real love don't work like that**. You shouldn't leave a visit feeling like **you're on top of the world** when you know deep down, he's just gonna **use your emotions** to get more from you. **Protect yourself**. Don't fall for the **illusion**. Those visits? They're just **another hustle**, and you need to wake up and see that for what it is.

You deserve **real connection**, **respect**, and **true love**, not someone who's just there for what they can get. **Don't get lost in the game**. **Recognize the hustle** before it drains you. And remember, **you're stronger than this**.

§9.4 The "I Need You" Card – How His Family Plays Your Loyalty

The Smoothest Manipulation in the Playbook

Girl, let me tell you something—they play you with that "I need you" card, and they play it smooth. It ain't just him—it's his whole family working together to use your loyalty against you. They know exactly how to make you feel like you're the only one who can save him, like you're the one who's gonna hold it all together while he's locked up. And that I need you talk? It's just another manipulation tactic.

Mama and the Emotional Button Push

You know the drill—mama calls you, all tearful, saying how hard it is on him, how much he misses you and needs you to keep holding him down. She'll even say things like, "I don't know what he'd do without you. You're the only one he trusts." Now you're feeling all important, thinking you're the one who can save him. But here's the reality: they know exactly how to push those emotional buttons. They make you feel like you're the rock in his life, the one who's going to make everything better, when really, you're just part of the game.

The Guilt Trap Setup

They'll hit you with the "I need you" line at the right moment, when you're emotionally vulnerable. You've been thinking about him, missing him, wanting to be there for him. And then bam, here comes mama or his cousin, saying, "He's so lost without you. If you don't help him, he'll fall apart." And just like that, you feel guilty. You think you have to keep sending to make sure he stays okay. You're not just sending because he needs help, you're sending because they've made you feel like it's your responsibility to keep him afloat.

But girl, you need to step back and see the truth. He don't need you to save him, he's just working you. And his family is right there with him, using your loyalty and your love as the perfect weapon to keep you giving.

They play the long game. It's not just about him, it's about his whole team—mama, sister, cousin, and even his boys on the outside—they all know how to use your heart against you. They're feeding you that guilt, making you think that if you stop giving, you're abandoning him. But you're not abandoning him—you're breaking free.

The Big Reveal – What Happens When You Step Back

Here's the kicker: when you finally step back, when you stop answering those guilt-trip calls and stop sending money and packages, you'll see the real play. They don't care about you, they care about what you can do for them. They're using your loyalty to keep you in the game, to make sure you keep sending money, love, and support. And the whole time, you think you're doing the right thing, when really, you're just another pawn in their hustle.

Keisha's Real Talk — Loyalty Ain't a Chain

Wake up. Don't let them play on your loyalty like that. Love ain't about guilt trips or making you feel responsible for someone else's actions. Real love doesn't use guilt to keep you locked in. If they really cared about you, they wouldn't be putting you in a position where you feel like you gotta keep giving just to prove your loyalty. You don't owe them shit.

You're more than just a source of income. Stop letting them make you feel like it's on you to keep the relationship going. You gotta protect your heart, and if that means stepping back, so be it. Let them figure their own shit out. You deserve someone who doesn't play on your loyalty but respects it.

§9.5 Devon's Family Hustle: Played From All Sides

Fooled by the Voice, Fooled by the Game

Devon had me fooled, no doubt. I thought it was just him—locked up, needing someone to hold him down, someone who'd support him while he was doing time. He'd call me on the phone, that sweet, deep voice telling me how much he missed me, how he couldn't wait to get out and make things right. I believed him. I wanted to believe him, so bad. But I wasn't just dealing with him, I was dealing with his whole family.

Mama Starts the Play

At first, it was just his mama. She'd call me, soft and sweet, asking how I was doing, telling me how much Devon loved me. She'd hit me with that "he's been through so much, baby" line, making me feel like I was the only one who could help him. "He's been in there too long," she'd say, "I don't know what he'd do without you."

I couldn't say no. I didn't want to. So I sent money, I sent care packages, I sent little notes—whatever I thought might keep him feeling loved. But it wasn't just Devon needing me. Mama was making sure that my pockets stayed open. Every time I'd send something, I'd get a text from her, "Thank you so much for helping my boy. He really needs it." I thought I was doing the right thing, being the good girlfriend, making sure he had everything he needed.

The Whole Family Eats

But that's where I messed up. It wasn't just him. It was the whole family hustle. When I started sending money, it wasn't just for Devon's commissary—it was for his sisters, his cousins, and his uncles. They all had a piece of the pie.

It was his sister next. She started texting me, too. Soft at first, asking how I was, checking in to see if I was still sending him what he needed. But then, she slid in with the requests—small stuff at first. "Hey, can you send a little extra this week? We need to get him some books for his case." And like a fool, I sent it. I thought I was helping. But I wasn't helping, I was being played.

Then his cousins started hitting me up. They'd ask for a little something here and there, "Hey, I'm trying to make sure Devon has some snacks. Can you send something for him?" They'd all work together, getting me hooked emotionally, making me feel like I was part of their family, like I was needed, like I was the one who could keep him going. But every time I'd send something, I'd realize more of the family was eating off me.

Devon Wasn't Innocent Either

And Devon? He wasn't innocent in this. He'd tell me how much he loved me, how much he needed me, how he'd be a better man once he got out. But I wasn't the only one he was telling that to. He'd say, "You're the only one who understands, baby, I need you to hold me down." But I could hear the same thing from his sister, his mama, his uncle. They were all playing me—working me over, getting me to give more.

One day, I caught him—his cousin's name popped up on his phone. I saw that familiar number again, and this time I didn't just ignore it. I opened the messages. There it was: "Hey, girl, we need some help this week. Devon's really going through it, we need more money for his case." They were all in it together. He wasn't just running the game—his whole family was working it. They'd pass messages, ask for more money, and when I'd give, they'd be thankful—acting like they were so grateful for my support. But they weren't grateful, they were using me.

The Cold Turkey Cut-Off

I wasn't just a girlfriend—I was the ATM, and they were all eating off me, all making me feel like I was doing it for Devon when really, I was just funding their lifestyle.

I was pissed, hurt, feeling like a damn fool. I realized that none of them were in it for me—they were using me to keep Devon comfortable. I thought I was helping him, but I was just feeding into the game. I was emotionally hooked, but it wasn't love, it was manipulation. And it wasn't just Devon—it was the entire family, playing their parts, each one making me feel like I was the one who could help while they kept taking.

I had to cut it. Cold turkey. I blocked his mama's number, his sister, his cousins. I stopped sending money, stopped answering their calls, stopped letting them play me.

Devon's family was a hustle, and I was just another pawn in the game. But when I finally stepped back and looked at the situation from the outside, I realized something important—I don't need him or his family to define my worth. I don't need anyone to play me, no matter how smooth their game is. I am my own strength. And I'm done being anyone's fool.

Keisha's Final Word — Protect Your Peace

Don't let them play you. You're not just here to support them financially, emotionally, and physically. Recognize the game before it drains you. If they really loved you, they wouldn't be using you like a resource. Know your worth, and don't let anyone make you feel like you're obligated to keep giving. Protect your peace and your money. Period.

§9.6 Raven Sinclair's Commentary

Families love to throw around words like *loyalty* and *blood*, but let me tell you — prison families rewrite the dictionary. Blood doesn't mean loyalty here, it means leverage. Mama ain't calling you because she loves you. She's calling because you're the new financial aid office, and she's running FAFSA for felons. Sister ain't texting you because she wants to be your homegirl. She's texting to keep you in line, keep you paying tuition into the family hustle.

You want to know the sickest part? Half the time, it doesn't even feel like manipulation — it feels like *acceptance*. They make you feel chosen, welcomed, "part of the family." And that's the real knife in the ribs, because who doesn't want to belong? Who doesn't want to believe they're saving someone's son, someone's brother, someone's cousin? They weaponize your empathy, then feed on it like vultures on a carcass.

I've been there. I believed the sweet talk from mama, the "thank yous" from sis, the tears over the phone. I thought it meant I was being brought into something sacred. What it really meant was that I was being brought into payroll. My role? ATM disguised as girlfriend. My reward? Guilt trips, empty promises, and an inbox full of "just a little more" requests.

Here's the truth, ladies: the *real family* ain't them — it's you and the women who finally woke up and saw through the bullshit. Because once you stop feeding the machine, the "family" vanishes quicker than his promises. They don't care about you — they care about the pipeline. And the second you turn off the faucet, the family reunion's over.

So stop mistaking guilt for love. Stop mistaking manipulation for loyalty. Blood might be thicker than water, but in this hustle? It's thinner than your damn bank account after they bled you dry.

§9.7 Larry Levine Commentary

Let's stop pretending mama's sweet tea and Sunday hugs got anything to do with this. That woman ain't praying for your happiness, she's praying you're dumb enough to keep Venmo'ing her son's ramen fund. And the sisters? Please. They're not your new besties, they're the HR department of this family-run scam — onboarding you, giving you the handbook, making sure you're fully trained before you start coughing up cash like a broken ATM.

You thought you were joining a family? Congratulations, you just joined Amway with commissary. Multi-level motherfucking marketing, except the only product moving is your self-respect. Mama sells you guilt, sis sells you validation, cousin sells you pity, and they all cash the same check — *yours*.

And here's the kicker: you think you're special because they "let you in." Newsflash — they let everybody in. You're not chosen, you're recruited. The only reason you feel like family is because they studied you like a manual. They know exactly which buttons to push: guilt if you hesitate, flattery if you doubt, tears if you start pulling away. It's not love, it's fucking strategy.

So let me give it to you straight: you're not ride-or-die, you're ride-or-dupe. You're not his partner, you're the family's group project, and they're all getting an A off your back. Mama, sis, cousin, even the lazy uncle who never did shit — they're all eating because you're stupid enough to keep feeding the pot.

You want out? Stop paying dues. Stop answering mama's guilt voicemails. Stop letting "family" talk to you like you're one of them. You're not. You're the mark. And the second you pull the plug, watch how fast "we love you, girl" turns into radio silence. That's the truth. That's the reality. And if it stings? Good. Maybe it'll finally slap you awake.

CHAPTER TEN

Legal Hustles

---

§10.1 – Emotional Manipulation to Legal Games

He Start with Love Because Money Would Be Too Obvious

Girl, these dudes don't open with "Can I get $50?" — they open with "You the only one who understands me." That's how they do it. Soft. Sweet. Slow. He start off soundin' like he read a relationship blog in Cell Block C. "I prayed for a woman like you." "You give me peace." "I feel seen." Baby, he see your **bank account**, not your soul. You think you're talkin' to a broken man with a good heart, but what you got is a bored manipulator with nothin' but time and a prepaid call schedule. He testin' the water to see if you bite. He ain't askin' for nothin' at first, just seein' if you'll text back quick. If you laugh at his little jail jokes. If you say "Awww" when he say, "You give me somethin' to live for." And when you do? Boom. Hook set. That's the openin' move in a very old, very dirty playbook.

You Ain't Support. You Payroll

Once he know you hooked, he flip the script. You don't even notice it at first. He still sayin' all the sweet shit, but now there's little asks attached. "Bae, my books low." "Bae, I need a copy of my transcript from the court." "Bae, you think you could call my lawyer?" Girl, how you go from meetin' this man online to runnin' errands for his freedom? You at home Googlin' legal terms like you in law school, sendin' money you don't even have, and callin' it love. That ain't love. That's logistics. You on his schedule. You takin' tasks. You **doing the job of three people** while he lay in a bunk scratchin' his nuts and feelin' important. He not buildin' a future with you. He usin' your free-world freedom to make his own time easier. And every time you try to set a boundary? He say you changin'. He say, "Everybody switch up on me, I thought you was different." Nah, he just mad you noticed you became his secretary.

That Legal Shit Ain't About Justice — It's About Control

Now here's where it get real dirty. The legal talk. The "My lawyer ain't shit" stories. The "If I had better representation I'd be out" line. He not tellin' you that 'cause he want you to understand his case. He tellin' you that to **get you involved in his case.** He plantin' the idea that you need to step in, because he can't do it alone. You send money to a lawyer you never met. You write letters to judges. You tell people he's innocent when you don't even know the full charge. That's not love, baby. That's a liability. He just shifted the weight of his conviction onto your back, and you carryin' it like it's a damn purse. And let me tell you something else — those letters you writing him? The ones where you pour your heart out? They ain't tucked under his pillow. They sittin' in a folder, ready to be used in court as proof he got "support." You not his girlfriend. You his **evidence.**

Once Mama Call You Baby, It's Too Late

This ain't a one-man hustle. Soon as his mama start callin' you "baby" and askin' how you doin', you already too deep. She part of it. So is the cousin. So is the sister. They all playin' their roles in this little play. They don't care about you — they care about what you're bringin' to the table. You the wallet. You the ride. You the outside connection. They butter you up just enough to keep you feelin' special while they pass your number around like it's a family heirloom. Now you hearin' from people you never met, all tellin' you how much your love means to him. Girl, he not tellin' them you his queen. He tellin' them you his **plug**. You payin' like you his wife, but you ain't even met him in real life. You cookin' meals and sendin' pictures like y'all married, but he readin' your messages in a cell full of other dudes laughin' at how he got you doin' more for him than he ever did for you.

If He Ain't Doin' Nothin' for You, You Bein' Used

Let me ask you something real simple — what's he doin' for you? Besides talkin'? Besides makin' you feel needed just enough to get what he want? 'Cause if all he givin' you is attention and all you givin' him is **everything else**, that ain't love. That's a transaction. He offerin' promises and pillow talk, and you payin' with money, time, energy, and your whole damn peace. Ain't no balance in that. Ain't no future in that. And every day you keep playin' along with it, the deeper you sink into a hole that gon' be real hard to crawl out of once your credit shot, your friends stop pickin' up the phone, and you look in the mirror and can't even recognize who the hell you became.

Keisha's Final Word: Stop Callin' It Love When It's a Fuckin' Scam

You not bein' loyal. You bein' tricked. You think you holdin' a man down, but really you holdin' him **up**, like a robbery. And the weapon he usin'? It's your heart. He know you got a soft spot, and he weaponizin' it. I ain't here to judge you. I've been you. I know what it feel like to believe the voice on the phone more than the life in front of you. But let me say this real slow — if he needs you broke, drained, stressed, and isolated to "prove" you love him, then you don't need that man. You need a reset. Don't let no jailhouse poet ruin your life out here in the real world. Wake the fuck up, and cut that motherfucker loose.

§10.2 – Power of Attorney: Controlling Your Finances and Assets

This Ain't Just About Love, It's About Access

Girl, lemme break this shit down real clear — when he starts talkin' about "power of attorney," that ain't about trust. That's about *access*. Access to your money. Access to your car. Access to your house. Access to your life. You think he just want help payin' for his appeal or signin' some papers for commissary? Nah, baby. He settin' up a whole-ass pipeline straight to your pockets. And the wildest part? He'll make it sound like *you're* the one in control — like you're "helpin' him handle business." But once that pen hits that paper, the *real* control is gone, and you won't even know it till you get hit with a bounced rent check.

Baby, I Just Need a Little Help With This Paperwork

That's how it starts. He hit you with the soft voice — "I trust you more than anybody out here, baby." He tell you you're his "rock," his "real one," and how everybody else done let him down. Next thing you know, you're sittin' in some notary office, signin' documents you barely read while he's on the phone tellin' you it's just some "legal formality." Girl. Stop right there. You think this man who lied about his *baby mama*, who hid his *other penpal*, who manipulates his *own mama* — you think he's tellin' you the *truth* about some legal paperwork? Come on now.

They Don't Want Support — They Want Control

Let me be clear — this ain't about support. This is about *control*. A power of attorney lets that man handle your money like it's his. He can sign contracts, pull funds, transfer titles, all in *your* name. And once he got that shit? He don't even need to *ask* you no more. Hell, I seen women get their whole stimulus check rerouted to a prepaid card they didn't even know existed. And who set it up? Their "man." Their "soulmate." Their damn *warden*.

If You Gotta Ask What It Is, You Don't Need to Sign It

Let me drop a little rule for life: *If you don't know what the hell it is, don't sign it.* Period. If he can't explain every word of that form without sayin' "just trust me," then he's hiding somethin'. That's not love — that's a hustle in legal clothes. A man that really care about you ain't gon' hand you documents that could ruin your life. And if he do? That ain't your man. That's a predator in prison-issued khakis.

You Gon' Be the One Left Holdin' the Bag

Guess what happens when he uses that power of attorney to fuck some shit up? You the one holdin' the bag. The creditors don't call *him*. The repo man don't show up to the prison. They comin' to *you*. To your house. To your job. They ain't gonna wanna hear "But I thought I was helpin' him." Baby, the law don't care. His name might be on the form, but your name is on the damn bill.

The Hustle Ain't Always Loud — Sometimes It's Signed and Notarized

This one ain't the loud, obvious hustle. It ain't sweet words and fake tears. It's paperwork. It's mail. It's fax machines and quiet scams that don't scream till it's too damn late. You think you bein' a good woman. You think you just helpin' your man handle business. But what you *really* doin'? You lettin' him play CEO of your damn life while you out here workin' doubles and overdraftin' at the grocery store. Wake up, girl.

§10.3 – The Illusion of the Legal Dream Team

Alright girl, lemme ask you somethin' — how many times he told you *"my legal team is on it"* like he got some high-powered attorney firm workin' around the clock for his case? You ever ask for a name? A business card? Hell, even a screenshot of an email? No? That's 'cause the only "legal team" he got is a half-literate cellie with a stolen typewriter ribbon and a GED. But he got you believin' he's got Johnny Cochran's ghost workin' appeals from the afterlife.

Jailhouse Lawyer = Google + Ego

These so-called jailhouse lawyers? Baby, most of 'em ain't lawyers. They're inmates who read two law books and now think they Clarence Darrow. They'll tell your man he got "constitutional violations," "Brady issues," and "ineffective assistance claims" — all buzzwords they half understand and weaponize to drag you into false hope. And guess who ends up payin' for all that bullshit paperwork they tryin' to file? **You.** With your last $200, thinkin' you payin' for justice, when really? You just buyin' printer ink and stamps for a fantasy case that's goin' nowhere.

The Mysterious "Outside" Paralegal

Now here come the next part of the circus — the *outside paralegal*. Girl, he gon' tell you his "cousin Tasha" work for some law office and she just needs a few bucks to file his appeal. First off, if she *really* was a paralegal, she wouldn't be askin' you for Zelle and CashApp like it's rent week. Second, every time you ask for a receipt or something legit? Silence. Excuses. "She busy right now." Nah baby, that's because **Tasha don't exist**, or if she do, she's playin' you and five other women at the same damn time.

The Paper Shuffle Game

They love to play the "paper shuffle." You'll get letters with "legal jargon," envelopes with "official" lookin' seals, maybe even some court documents. But pay attention — those case numbers? Don't match. The judge's name? Spelled wrong. And the grammar? Girl, if the commas look confused, it's because the whole thing's a printout from *How to Fool a Good Woman Dot Com*. He's banking on you bein' too overwhelmed to question any of it.

False Hope Is the Real Scam

This whole game ain't just about money — it's about **hope**. That's the currency. If he can sell you on the dream that he's innocent, that he's fightin', that he just needs a little help to beat the system? You'll keep showin' up. You'll keep sendin' checks. You'll keep tellin' your friends and family he's "different." And every time he gets you to believe in that fake-ass legal dream? That's another win for him, and another loss for your bank account and your peace of mind.

Don't Let the Law Be Another Lie

Listen, sis — if your man *really* got legal help, you'll see names, bar numbers, legit invoices. You won't be gettin' scribbled notes on notebook paper signed by "Attorney R.J." with no return address. If you see *more hustle than help*, that ain't a legal strategy — that's a damn con.

§10.4 – When It All Falls Apart: Excuses, Blame & the Vanishing Act

The "You Fucked Up My Case" Play

Let me be real clear, sis. If you helped this man with anything legal — sent money, typed up letters, printed forms, even just made a few calls — best believe he gon' flip it back on you the second shit don't go his way. He'll say *you did it wrong, you filed it late, you sent it to the wrong place.* You gon' sit there confused, thinkin' you helped, when in his mind? You just became the reason his fake-ass appeal got "denied."

It's the ultimate gaslight move. You tryin' to save him, and now suddenly **you** the villain in his little jailhouse soap opera. Ain't that a bitch?

From "Queen" to Scapegoat

You went from "my rock," "my queen," "the only one I trust" to *"You don't understand the system!"* overnight. That switch flips fast as hell once the fantasy falls apart. He need somebody to blame, and he sure as hell ain't about to point that finger at his jailhouse lawyer crew or them shady ass paralegals that never existed. Nope — he points it straight at the chick who loved him enough to believe his bullshit.

The Ghost Protocol

Once the money dries up or the appeal gets denied for the 15th time, you know what happens next, right? He disappears. Calls slow down. Emails get short. That "I love you forever" energy turns into "I need some space to figure things out." Baby, ain't no space — he just movin' on to the next chick who ain't caught on yet.

He ghosts you like a damn poltergeist, and if you *do* hear from him, it's gonna be some sad-ass letter about how he's depressed and "needs time to heal." Girl, heal from what? You paid for everything, did all the work, and now he too emotionally exhausted to even say thank you?

He Already Got a Backup

Here's the part that really burns — while you sittin' at home cryin', wonderin' what the hell went wrong, he already groomin' the next one. That's why the excuses started poppin' up weeks before the crash. "Phone privileges messed up." "Mail ain't goin' out." "My celly lost my list." Nah, boo. He was just switchin' lanes without usin' a blinker.

Your Wake-Up Call

This is where you gotta get up off that emotional floor and **see it for what it is**. The whole setup was never about justice. It was survival for him, and manipulation for you. You were a chess piece, not a partner. You were a wallet with feelings.

And now? You're done. Not broken — done. That's a **damn difference**.

§10.5 Devon's Legal Hustle

Holding Him Down — Or So I Thought

I thought I was doing the right thing. Devon was locked up, and I was holding him down like any good girl would. Writing those letters, sending him those care packages, keeping his head in the game while he was stuck behind bars. We had plans, you know? He was always talking about how he was gonna get out, how we'd start fresh, how everything would be different. And I believed him.

But it didn't take long before I realized I wasn't just supporting him emotionally—I was funding his whole damn life. It started off small, just a little bit of money for his commissary here, a lawyer's fee there. But then it escalated, like I didn't even see it coming.

The Hook: "I Need You" and the Legal Card

He started talking more about his appeals, about how he needed better legal help, about how the court system screwed him over. And every time I picked up the phone, it was "I need you, baby", "I can't do this without you", and I was hooked. Every call, every letter, he made me feel like I was the only one who truly understood him—like I was the only one who could help him get out.

And I believed it. I wanted to believe it.

That's when they pulled the first move—the Power of Attorney. Devon asked me for a favor, just one little favor, he said. "Baby, I need you to sign this. It's just some legal stuff, to get my case moving. You're the only one who can do this for me. You're the only one who understands what I'm going through." I didn't even think twice. He was asking for a little bit of trust and some help. I didn't think it was a big deal, so I signed it. Just like that. But that signature? That was the hook.

Legal Chains and Family Pressure

Once I signed, I realized I had just given him control—legal control over everything. My bank accounts, my credit, everything. He wasn't just fighting a legal battle; he was using me to finance his freedom. The hustle was on, and I was caught up in it. I was sending money, paying for lawyers, helping him with his appeals, all while thinking I was doing the right thing. But Devon wasn't working to get out—he was using me to stay comfortable while he was locked up.

Then, it got even slicker. The family got involved. Mama started calling more often, asking for money, asking for legal support. She'd tell me how much Devon loved me, how much he needed me. She'd say things like, "He's doing this for us, baby, for the future we're gonna have. Just a little more help, that's all we need." And I kept giving, thinking I was helping him build a future, not realizing I was funding a system that was only benefiting him and his family.

The Marriage Trap

Then came the talk of marriage. Suddenly, Devon was talking about how important it was for us to get married. "I need you, baby. We're gonna make it. We need to do this now, before I get out. You're the only one who's got my back. I want us to have a future, together." At first, I thought it was romantic, but then it hit me—this wasn't about love. This was about control. Marriage wasn't a promise of forever—it was a way for him to get access to my assets, my finances, and my future. He wasn't thinking about building a life with me; he was thinking about locking me down legally so he could keep using me for everything I had.

I didn't realize it at first, but when I started thinking about it, I saw the game. The marriage wasn't about building love, it was about locking me in. The second I said yes, everything I had was at risk. He had control over my money, my property, and everything else we shared. And it didn't stop there—his family kept pushing for me to sign the papers, saying things like, "You know he can't do this without you, right?" But it wasn't about us—it was about making sure he had access to everything I owned.

The Back-Up Plan — Divorce as Another Hustle

But here's the kicker—the minute we separated, or even started thinking about divorce? That was his back-up plan. If things went south, Devon and his family knew exactly what to do—they'd use the divorce to claim my stuff, to get spousal support, to take what I had worked for while he sat back and let me pay the price for his legal battles. It was all part of the plan.

I had to wake up. I had to see the game for what it really was. Devon wasn't in love with me—he was in love with the hustle. He was using me to keep his life comfortable, using my money to fund his future. And I was letting him. The family hustle? It was all connected. They were using emotional manipulation, legal control, and even marriage to keep me locked in.

Keisha's Final Word — Protect Yourself

Girl, don't get played. Marriage, legal control, it's all part of the hustle to keep you emotionally tied and financially responsible. Don't fall for it. Know your worth, know your boundaries, and don't let anyone use your loyalty as a way to take what you've worked for. Protect yourself. It's time to take back control.

§10.6 Raven's Commentary

Let me tell you something straight, from one woman to another — *love should never require a law degree and a damn notary stamp to survive.*

Everything Keisha laid out in this chapter? I've seen it. Hell, I've *lived* it. You start out thinking you're just helping your man navigate the system. You believe in him, in his fight, in his *story*. You feel like you're standing by your man through the worst chapter of his life.

But what you don't see — until it's too damn late — is that *you're not part of the story*. You're part of the *strategy*.

That "appeal" you're bankrolling? Probably written by some jailhouse lawyer hustling twenty other women just like you. That "legal team" he swears he's building? Might be three convicts and a busted typewriter. And those "important forms" he's asking you to print, mail, notarize, and overnight? Half of them never even leave the envelope once they hit the mailroom. This isn't love. It's logistics. It's manipulation dressed up like loyalty.

And let's not ignore the worst part — the psychological warfare. The way he flips your help into his failure. The way *you* become the reason things fell apart. That's not accountability. That's a con.

Keisha put it best: **you were never the queen, you were the pawn.**

So here's my advice to you now that you've read Chapter 10: Don't just *read* it — *believe* it. Internalize it. Let it piss you off. Let it sharpen your instincts. Because you're not just fighting heartbreak — you're fighting a system of lies wrapped in prison mail. And if you're still in it — if you're still second-guessing what's real and what's not — let me make it easy for you: If you're doing more for his freedom than he is? **It's not love. It's labor.** And you deserve better.

§10.7 Larry Levine Commentary

Let me make this real clear—if you read this chapter and still think you're helping some misunderstood man fight the system, I got bad news for you: you're not a girlfriend. You're a fucking tool. Not the kind in his box either—the kind he uses to file bullshit appeals, move dirty money, and "stand by his side" while he orchestrates a full-blown puppet show with you on the strings.

These prison love hustles don't stop at commissary and fake tears—they graduate. And Chapter 10 is where the scam gets sophisticated. It's where the lies stop being "I love you" and start being "Baby, we need to retain counsel." Let that sink in. By the time you hit this point in the con, your man's not just running game—he's running a fucking legal campaign, and you're the only idiot writing checks, printing documents, and overnighting envelopes like some ride-or-die Amazon Prime account.

You wanna know how deep it goes? Ask yourself this: ever paid a "legal fee" through CashApp to a guy named "Big Meech Paralegal Services"? Ever been asked to send discovery paperwork to someone you've never spoken to? Ever cried on the phone while he screamed at you for not understanding "how the legal system works"? If so, congratulations—you've been promoted from side piece to secretary. And you damn sure didn't sign up for that job.

Here's the part that'll piss you off most—he knew what he was doing the whole damn time. Every motion? Planned. Every deadline? Weaponized. Every fake lawyer on the other end of that collect call? Scripted. This ain't chaos. This is strategy. And you? You're the fucking infantry in a war he ain't never planned on winning.

So if you're still out here calling yourself a "down chick," guess what—you're down bad. You're out here chasing justice for a man who don't even chase truth. You're begging the system to be fair while he's using you to manipulate the fuck outta it.

Wake up. The only thing getting freed in this situation is your time, your money, and your sanity—right out the damn window. This ain't about loyalty. This is about self-preservation. So close this chapter, look in the mirror, and ask yourself: Am I in love? Or am I in litigation with a side of delusion?

Because if the answer ain't crystal clear—you're already the next cautionary tale.

The Fallout & Escape

What These Modules Cover

By Module 4, the glitter's gone and the mask has slipped. The fantasy of "forever" rots into excuses, false promises of freedom, and manipulative silence. This ain't about love anymore — it's about survival, and whether you finally walk the fuck away. These chapters strip down the final stages of the hustle: when he's out, when he's silent, and when you're left holding the weight of a future that never existed.

CHAPTER 11 – The Freedom Fantasy

He swears the dream starts the day he walks out the gate. Houses, jobs, marriage, forever. Bullshit. He don't leave prison behind — he brings prison with him, and you become his resource on the outside. The so-called "fresh start" is just another round of manipulation, dressed up as redemption.

CHAPTER 12 – The Silent Treatment

When he ain't yelling, he's vanishing. Silence ain't peace — it's punishment. He disappears to make you chase, blame yourself, and hand him more power. Every unanswered call, every ignored message, is a leash. This chapter is where the illusion dies — where you finally stop apologizing to the void and reclaim your damn voice.

CHAPTER 13 - The Next Steps

This is the wake-up call nobody wants but everybody needs. Keisha and Raven burn down every excuse left, tearing apart the fairytale that kept women chained to prison hustlers. It's not about love — it's about control, manipulation, and the courage to finally walk the hell away. Larry ends it like a gunshot to denial: stop funding fantasies and reclaim your damn power.

The Real Takeaway

Module 4 is the breaking point. It's where you realize "freedom" is a fantasy, silence is a weapon, and you've been carrying dead weight long enough. This is the pivot: you either keep financing his lies, or you burn the whole circus down and walk away.

There's no soft landing here — just a hard truth: **he was never your future. He was your lesson.**

CHAPTER ELEVEN

The Freedom Fantasy

§11.1 Freedom and Why It's All Smoke and Mirrors

The Sweet Lie

Let's get this shit straight from the jump: **freedom after prison is a straight-up lie**. You ever heard the phrase, "When he gets out, it's a new beginning"? Yeah, *that's the bait*. They paint the picture like it's some fairytale, like once he steps out that gate, you two gonna be living like the *ideal couple*—walking hand-in-hand down a beach, champagne in hand, all happy and free. Fuck that.

That "freedom"? It's **smoke and mirrors**, plain and simple. They sell it to you like it's the golden ticket, like your whole life's gonna be rainbows and unicorns the minute he steps outta that prison. But I'm here to tell you that shit's just the **first part of the hustle**. The second he gets out, he's not stepping into freedom, he's stepping into a **bigger cage**. That's right. It's bigger, but it's still a damn cage. He might be wearing civilian clothes, but his mind? His mind is still locked up in survival mode. And what's worse? He's already plotting how to **use you** to make that so-called freedom look just like his old game on the outside.

You're Not Living the Dream, You're Living the Fantasy

You think the freedom starts when that prison door opens? Hell no. That's when the **real manipulation** kicks in. They want you to think it's a "new beginning," that it's all about new jobs, a new house, a new life.

You think that man's been sitting in a cell, reflecting on life, thinking about how he's gonna be a better partner to you? Nah. He's been sitting in that cell figuring out his **next hustle**, and the minute he walks free, you're gonna find yourself caught up in that same damn game.

You thought you were about to build a fresh future? Baby girl, you're about to be his **partner in crime**, whether it's financial, emotional, or worse. He's got plans, and they don't involve just loving you—they involve using you. You might be dreaming about a better life, but he's been dreaming about how he's gonna **cash in** on that dream and have you playing catch-up with the bills, the responsibilities, and the stress.

Survival Mode: He's Still in Prison, Mentally

Listen, no matter what, the system never really lets a man go free. He might be walking in the streets, but mentally? He's still locked in survival mode. Prison ain't just a physical cage—it's a damn mental prison, too. So you're thinking, *he's out, we can start over*. But what you don't see is the **residual trauma** he's carrying with him. Prison teaches you to survive, not to thrive. It teaches you how to manipulate, how to hustle, how to adapt, and guess what? He's not leaving that behind when he's released. That mentality sticks like a second skin.

The truth is, you're thinking you're about to start a new life together, but he's thinking he's about to **survive the outside** just like he survived inside. The difference? On the outside, you're his **resource**. You're the key to his survival, the one thing he knows he can manipulate to keep the wheels turning. And while you're imagining the fresh start, he's already setting you up to help fund the next stage of his hustle.

The Hustle Is Alive and Well – Don't Be Fooled

You ever notice how a lot of these dudes know how to talk the talk when they're locked up? They've had years to think up the perfect lines to get women wrapped around their fingers. When they get out, they don't forget those lines—they perfect them. He's not just thinking about starting over; he's thinking about **how he's gonna work the system**, how he's gonna **manipulate you**, and how he's gonna turn your loyalty into his next payoff.

And here's where it really gets ugly: by the time you start questioning the "dream," by the time you wake up and see the hustle for what it is, it's too damn late. He's already got his game plan locked down, and you're caught

CON GAMES & BROKEN HEARTS

in the middle of it. You thought you were building a future together? Nah, you were just the **stepping stone** to his next level of manipulation.

The Illusion of Freedom – It's a Script He's Been Running

The most dangerous part of this whole situation is the illusion of freedom. He'll sell you this dream, this *idea*, of how you're gonna be living it up. But at the core, that's all it is: a **fantasy**. He's going to tell you all the things you want to hear:

> "I can't wait to start over with you."
> "We're gonna make it, I swear."
> "We've been through too much to fail now."

And in the beginning, it feels real. It feels like everything's going your way. But all that shit is **hollow**, girl. It's just **another part of the hustle** to get you on board and keep you emotionally and financially locked in. Because once you're hooked, the real work begins—and that work? It's him **playing you** until you realize the game is over.

The Real Truth: You're Caught in the Next Round

You think you're escaping? Nah, sis. You're just **entering the next round** of the hustle. The real "freedom" starts when you finally take off those rose-colored glasses and see this for what it is. He's not out here trying to live free—he's out here looking for the next **opportunity to manipulate** you. The freedom he's really after? It's **your bank account, your time, your emotional energy, your resources**.

And once you realize that, it's already too late. He's already working you into a corner. You've bought into the fantasy so deep, it's hard to untangle yourself. You thought you were helping him, but all along, he's been **using you** as the ticket to his next con.

The Harsh Reality: Freedom Ain't Free, and You Ain't the One Living It

So, you thought that the minute he got out, everything would be better? You thought the fantasy of "freedom" was gonna work out the way it looked on paper? You weren't wrong—just **misled**. That freedom? It's a lie. And if you keep holding on to it, it's gonna cost you more than you can afford. Because you've been sold a dream, and that dream doesn't come with a return policy.

You are the one left holding the bag, baby. He'll be free, but you'll be paying the price. You're about to realize that the **real freedom** is walking away from the fantasy—because in the end, you're the one who's been locked in the cage.

§11.2 How They Sell You the Dream of Life After Release

Spinning the Fantasy with Empty Words

Girl, this is where the hustle gets real slick. When he's locked up, it's the perfect setup for them to **sell you a dream**. They've got time on their hands—time to *think* of the perfect lines to tell you. They know exactly what buttons to push, and they'll hit each one with precision. Every word that comes out their mouth is designed to keep you hooked, emotionally invested, and on the hook for their next move.

It starts simple—*"When I get out, we'll get a place. I'll get a job. We'll be a family. We're gonna live our best life, baby."* Sounds innocent, doesn't it? Sounds like he's planning for a real future with you, right? WRONG. That's the dream he's selling you. You think he's been working on a better version of himself, on a better future for you both. Nah, baby. He's been cooking up ways to make you believe in that future while he's plotting how to make you **pay** for it once he gets out.

The Plan – What He's Really Thinking

And let me break it down: you might even get a whole-ass plan. He'll talk about **where you'll live, what car you'll drive, vacations you'll take**. He might even throw out **dates**—like the first month after he's out, the first year. He paints the perfect picture of a couple with nothing but potential. And in your mind, you start building a future around that. You start thinking about how you'll finally be able to leave the past behind, build a better life, live the kind of life you **deserve**. You're thinking about **sunsets, romantic dinners, new beginnings**—the fairy tale.

But here's the catch: He ain't building shit. He's not planning for a future with you—he's planning for how he's gonna use **you** to fund his future. While you're over there dreaming about that house, he's got his eye on your **bank account**, your **bills**, your **loyalty**. That dream he's selling you? It's his **escape plan**—and you're the one who's gonna pay for it.

The Long Con – Making You Fund His Fantasy

Don't be fooled, girl. That whole "we're gonna be a family" line? That's not about him building with you. It's about him building **his life with you** paying for it. He knows exactly what to say to keep you **emotionally invested**, to make you feel like **you're in this together**. But in reality, he's thinking about how to keep you paying the rent, keeping the utilities on, sending him commissary money, and covering his bills while he figures out how to make the life he promised you happen.

You think he's working on his "rehabilitation" while he's locked up? Nah. He's working on his **hustle**. He's figuring out how he's gonna play you into paying for this dream that **only he benefits from**. You're thinking about that house, that car, that vacation—you're thinking about all the things he's promised you—while he's thinking about how he's gonna get you to take care of everything while he takes his sweet time to come through with a plan **that will never happen**.

The Fantasy Is All on Your Dime

And here's where it gets ugly. He gets out, right? Now the real manipulation starts. He'll be all charming, sweet, throwing around all that "we'll make it together" talk. But that talk will be followed by actions—or should I say *inactions*? He'll drag his feet getting a job, he'll rely on you to pay the rent for a few months, he'll *talk* about doing things and "getting on track," but you'll be the one picking up the slack. The **dream** will turn into a *living nightmare* where you're the one putting in all the work while he's still running the same hustle from the inside, just with a new set of clothes.

The Biggest Hustle – Your Mind, Your Money, Your Time

It's not just the money, girl. It's your time, it's your heart. The real con is how he convinces you that you need him in your life, how he convinces you that your future is tied to him. You'll end up sacrificing your time, your energy, your plans—all to prop up **his** dream, and in the end, you'll realize that dream was always about him **using you** to build **his** life. You were the *mule* in the story—

the one working hard to make his vision happen, and you didn't even know you were signing up for it.

The Illusion of Change – Same Game, New Set-Up

But that's the lie. He's not trying to change. The plan? Same game, new set-up. He's just making you believe this time it'll be different. When you start questioning things—when you start seeing the cracks in his story—he'll throw out the "I love you"s again, the "we're a team" talk, the "we're gonna make it together" speeches. But the truth? He's already got a backup plan. He's already working on the next step of the hustle, and if you're not careful, **you'll be the one left picking up the pieces** when it all falls apart.

He's going to keep you caught in the same damn cycle, and while you're dreaming about the "perfect life," he's already planning how to use your loyalty to get exactly what he wants. That **new start**? It's a trap, babe. And you're the one funding it.

The Wake-Up Call – It's Time to See the Game for What It Is

It's time to **wake up**. You've been sold a dream that doesn't exist. He's using your loyalty, your love, and your hope to trap you in a hustle you didn't sign up for. That fantasy of life after prison? It's built on lies. The only way out is to stop believing in the dream and start living in the **real world**—the one where **you** come first, where your goals and your dreams don't revolve around fixing him or building his future.

That "new beginning" you're hoping for? Stop waiting for it, because it's **never coming**. And if you keep playing into this game, you're going to find yourself stuck in a cycle of broken promises and endless disappointment. It's time to **break the fantasy**—and if you don't, you're going to find yourself stuck in a lie that's been building since day one. The **freedom** you're looking for starts when you stop letting him sell you that dream.

§11.3 Why That Future Doesn't Exist

The Sweet Talk – "We'll Build This Together"

You've heard it before, girl. The same tired lines wrapped in a sweet, seductive promise: *"We'll make it together. I need you to make it through."* He'll tell you how he's "changed," how he's "learned from his mistakes," how you're the one who can stop him from going back to his old ways. You're gonna be his **rock**, right? His **ride or die**? You'll be the one who keeps him grounded while he turns his life around, **together**, hand in hand, facing the world.

But **let me tell you** something—**that's all smoke and mirrors.** He's not trying to build with you, girl. **He's trying to use you.**

The Real Game – A Co-Signer for His Bullshit

You think it's a partnership? Nah. You're just a **co-signer for his bullshit**. You're the one who'll hold it down financially, emotionally, physically—**while he does what?** He does the same shit he's been doing behind those prison walls. The same manipulation, the same hustle, the same "woe-is-me" stories. All he's really doing is looking for someone to bankroll his fresh start when he gets out. He knows you've got a heart bigger than your wallet, and he's gonna tap into that love until it's running on fumes.

You're out here trying to be the strong, supportive partner, while he's over there scheming on how to keep you locked in his game. The minute he walks out that gate, the game starts again—and this time, you're footing the bill.

The Trap – Same Hustle, Different Stage

This "we'll make it together" fantasy? It's just another round of the same hustle he's been running in prison. **Nothing changes.** He's not trying to build a future with you, he's just setting you up to be the one who carries his weight when his old life crumbles again. You're supposed to be the foundation of his "new life," right? But the truth is, **he's still living in survival mode**, and he's gonna drag you down with him until you can't breathe.

You'll be thinking you're making progress, thinking you're working toward something better, when in reality, you're stuck in the same toxic cycle, *just with a different title*. He'll keep playing the same game, running the same hustle, and you'll be left holding the bag.

The New Hustle – A Fresh Start on Your Dime

You're thinking, "We'll make it. He's finally out, he's finally free. We'll get a place, he'll get a job, we'll build this life together." But what you don't see is that he's got a **new hustle**. The game has changed, but **he hasn't**. He's still the same man, with the same manipulative tricks, only now he's got **you** to bankroll his "fresh start."

While you're putting your energy into making this work—paying bills, covering his ass, managing the chaos—he's already moving to the next phase of his hustle. He's plotting his next move, the next woman, the next scam to keep you in the loop. You're carrying his weight, both emotionally and financially, while he's running the same play he's been running all along.

The "Future Together" – It Doesn't Exist

Let's be real, girl: the **"future together"** you've been dreaming of? It's a damn **illusion**. He'll keep selling you that same bullshit about building a life together, but all he's really doing is keeping you hooked into his game. He's promising you a future where the two of you are happy and stable, but in reality, he's already planning the next phase of his hustle—and you're the one funding it.

You think the end goal is a home, a family, a fresh start—but he's already looking at how to *milk you* for the next few years. He's not building with you. He's building **his future** on **your dime**. And when you start to realize that, it's already too late. He's already pulled you into the next round of the hustle, and you're left wondering how you got sucked into this game again.

The Hard Truth – You're Not His Partner, You're His Mark

The hardest truth you need to face? **You're not his partner, you're his mark**. You're the one who's been roped into the dream, the one who's been sold the story that **he's going to change**, that **this time is different**. But nothing's different. Nothing changes. He's still the same man, running the same scams, looking for the same thing: someone to take care of him when his old life falls apart.

That "we'll make it together" talk? It's just a way for him to keep you invested long enough to get what he wants. And when he gets what he wants, you'll be the one left holding the bag, paying the price for his new life while he moves on to the next hustle.

The Only Way Out – Breaking the Fantasy

Here's the deal, sis: the only way out is to stop believing the fantasy. **Stop buying into the idea** that he's going to change, that the two of you are going to build a future together. **He's already playing you**, and you've been so wrapped up in the dream that you can't see the game.

If you want real freedom, you need to break free from the illusion he's selling. **Stop making excuses for him**, stop believing in the fairy tale, and start living for **yourself**. This "we'll make it together" dream? It doesn't exist. And the longer you hold on to it, the more you're going to lose. **The real future** is one where you're free from his game, free from the fantasy, and free to live for yourself.

§11.4 How to Break Free from the Fantasy

The Hard Truth – Breaking the Illusion

Here it is, girl—**the hard truth**: the only way to break free from this damn fantasy is to **shatter it**. You've been living in a dream world, sold a lie wrapped up in sweet words and promises. It's time to see it for what it really is: a **fantasy built on your hope and his manipulation**. You've been thinking it's love, thinking it's real, but now you gotta see it for the hustle it is. You've been **played**.

Moving forward means **you** gotta make the move. Stop waiting for him to change, stop waiting for him to "get it together." That's just another way to keep you **stuck** in the past, circling back to the same damn lie. You gotta walk away from all that shit. Cut the ties. Break free from the emotional chains you've been wearing, thinking they were keeping you close, when they were really holding you down. It ain't gonna be easy, but it's gotta be done if you want **real freedom**.

The Fantasy's Foundation – Your Hope, His Hustle

Let's break it down: everything you've been believing in was built on **your hope** and his **hustle**. He's been selling you this dream, feeding you all these promises, and you've been eating it up like a starving person. The "we'll make it together" line? That's just another way for him to keep you **invested**—emotionally, financially, spiritually—in his game.

You're thinking about how things could be, about what the future holds, about how good it'll feel when he gets out and you two finally **start fresh**. He's thinking about **how he's gonna keep playing you** for everything you've got while he works on whatever scam he's got cooking next. You're stuck dreaming while he's making moves—and the worst part? You don't even see how deep the manipulation goes.

Cutting the Emotional Ties – No More Waiting

It's time to **cut the emotional ties**, girl. You can't keep waiting for **when he gets out**, waiting for him to magically transform into the person you thought he was or the man you hoped he'd become. That's a fool's game. He's not the one you thought he was. And the longer you keep believing in that illusion, the longer you're wasting your time and energy on a man who **can't give you real promises**. He's out here making moves for himself—while you're stuck waiting, giving your love, your time, your money, and your patience to someone who isn't going to change.

You've put your life on pause for this man long enough. It's time to **move forward**—and that means putting your life first. No more living for him. No more waiting for the man who promises everything but delivers nothing. Your goals, your peace, your future—they come first now. If he was really about the future, he would've been making those moves long before he got out. He wouldn't have used you as his backup plan.

Living for Yourself – The Only Way Out

It's time to stop believing in the **"we'll make it together"** fantasy. That shit doesn't exist. The future you've been imagining—where you two ride off into the sunset together, hand-in-hand, living your best life—isn't coming. The sooner you realize that, the sooner you can start living for **yourself** again.

You are what matters. *Your* future is what matters. And if he can't be part of that in a real way—if he can't match the energy, the effort, the love you're putting out—then he doesn't deserve to take up space in your world. You've been living in his game for too long, and it's time to flip the script.

Real Freedom – Walking Away from the Game

Real freedom isn't just about him getting out—it's about **you walking away** from the game. You've been living in a fantasy, thinking your worth was tied to him, thinking your future was connected to his release. But that's not it, sis. **Your worth** is tied to your own strength, your own ability to stand up, face the truth, and take control of your life.

The minute you decide to leave that fantasy behind and start living for yourself? **That's when you'll really be free.** Not because he's out of prison, but because you're no longer trapped in his web.

You're the one who holds the keys to your life. You're the one who decides what happens next. And once you realize that? You'll see that everything you've been waiting for was already within you. The freedom was always there—you just had to stop letting him run the show.

The Final Push – No More Looking Back

Now it's time to **look ahead**. You've been stuck in the past, dreaming about a future that was never real. It's time to step out of that fantasy and into your own reality. A reality where **you** come first, where **your happiness** isn't tied to someone else's drama, and where your future is something you build for yourself.

It won't be easy. It won't be quick. But you've got the power to make it happen. The moment you stop believing in that "together forever" fantasy is the moment you stop giving your energy to someone who's not willing to build a future with you.

Real freedom is waiting for you. And it starts with **walking away** from the game.

Keisha's Final Word – Don't Be the Fool Twice

Listen, girl—prison love ain't romance, it's a hustle with lipstick on it. Don't let him keep you locked up in a cage he built with his words. If a man's freedom is built on draining your pockets, your patience, and your peace, then that ain't freedom—that's you doing time right alongside him.

You wanna know what real love looks like? It don't cost you your sanity, it don't bleed your bank account, and it sure as hell don't leave you begging for scraps of respect. Real love builds you up. His shit just breaks you down.

So here's the advice: **don't wait for him to change—change your own damn life.** Walk away while you still got gas in your tank. Stop investing in his lies and start stacking for your future. 'Cause the minute you stop being his mark? That's the minute you finally get free.

§11.5 Raven Commentary

Let's get something straight real quick: Chapter 11 ain't here to soothe your feelings. It's here to rip the blindfold off and leave it on the prison floor.

If you didn't feel Keisha's rage in this one, you're numb. Dead in the heart. Because this ain't just a story—it's a warning wrapped in a confession. A raw, gut-level purge from a woman who loved a man deep in the system and damn near lost herself trying to hold him down. She poured her loyalty into a man who was pouring lies right back.

Devon didn't just hustle her—he rewrote her entire identity. Made her question her instincts, her sanity, her worth. And the part that cut the deepest? **She saw it coming.** Deep down, she knew. But that's the power of manipulation—it doesn't just lie to you, it makes *you* lie to *yourself*.

This chapter isn't just for the ones still stuck in it—it's for the ones who got out but haven't healed. For the women who still beat themselves up for "being stupid." You weren't stupid. **You were targeted.** Groomed. Worn down. Made to believe that being loyal meant being silent, compliant, and broke.

And now? Now she's done being silent. Now she's telling the truth so loud it echoes.

This is the part where we stop pretending it was love. It was survival—for him. And for her? It was almost destruction. Until she took her story back.

If that don't hit you in the chest, maybe you ain't ready for real healing yet. But when you are? Come back and read Chapter 11 again.

And this time? **Believe every word**

§11.6 Larry Levine Commentary

Let's not sugar-coat a goddamn thing—Chapter 11 is where the gloves come off and the illusion gets kicked square in the teeth. This ain't no "maybe he changed" love story. This is the part where reality shanks the fairytale in the ribs and keeps it movin'.

Keisha didn't write this to make you feel good. She didn't write it to be inspirational. She wrote it because she's done being played—and she's sick of watching other women get dragged down the same fucked-up path. She aired the kind of dirty truth most people die with stuck in their throat. That kind of raw pain? That's the shit you earn. Not from books, but from bleeding in real time while some smooth-talking inmate turns your loyalty into his power source.

Devon wasn't just a liar. He was a *fucking architect of delusion*. He built a fantasy and handed Keisha the blueprint, telling her it was a love story when it was really just a cage. A financial leash. A pipeline of support, sex, sympathy, and silence—all to keep **him** afloat while **she** sank.

And don't get it twisted—Keisha ain't stupid. None of the women who fall into this game are. They're *targeted*. Handpicked for their empathy, their loyalty, their wounds. It's always the women who've survived some shit already. The ones who know how to fight, but who still hope for love. And the system? It loves this setup. Because every minute you're wrapped up in his drama, you ain't building your own damn life. You're stuck. Emotional prison outside the bars.

Chapter 11 ain't entertainment—it's a **survival guide written in blood**. It's Keisha ripping the mask off the man she once would've died for and showing you what's underneath. And what's under there? Ain't nothing but rot. Lies. Excuses. Half-truths sprinkled with just enough affection to keep you dancing on the string. Every "I'm sorry," every "I didn't mean to," every "you're the only one" is a calculated line. A trap disguised as tenderness.

And yeah—she's angry. She's bitter. She's fucking *furious*. And guess what? She earned that rage. She earned the right to spit every syllable without apology, because she paid for it in years, in dollars, in dignity. And now she's reclaiming all of it in your face, whether you can handle it or not.

So here's the part where I talk to *you*, the reader. If you made it through this chapter and still got even an ounce of sympathy for the Devon in your life, then I got bad news: you're still under the spell. Still in the grip of a con you refuse to call a con. And the longer you stay there, the more pieces of yourself you give away until one day—boom—you wake up and don't even recognize the woman in the mirror.

This chapter isn't just a turning point in the book. It's supposed to be a turning point in *you*.

So yeah, it's harsh.
 Yeah, it stings.
 And yeah—it's the truth.

If you can't take it, you ain't ready to be free. And if you *can* take it? Then let this chapter be the funeral for every lie you've swallowed in the name of love.

No prayers.
 No eulogies.
 Just a closed casket for that bullshit.

CHAPTER TWELVE

The Silent Treatment

§12.1 – Emotional Manipulation at Its Fuckin' Finest

Let's keep it one hundred—this ain't no "he needs space" bullshit. This is *intentional silence* used like a fuckin' weapon. At first, it's just a few hours. Then it's a day. Then it's four days of you starin' at your phone like it's a damn Ouija board. You keep telling yourself, *"He just need time."* Nah, baby. He needs control—and you just handed it to him.

That silence? That ain't peace. It's punishment. And you feel it, deep. Every hour that goes by, you start pickin' yourself apart like *you* the problem. *"Did I say somethin' wrong? Did I text too much? Was I too needy?"* No, girl. You were just expectin' basic human decency, and that's too much for a manipulative motherfucker who gets off on watchin' you squirm.

It's psychological warfare—prison edition. These dudes can't throw hands behind bars, so they throw silence. And every second they stay quiet, they build that tension in your head. You start chasin'. You send that "Just checking on you" text. You call. You apologize for shit you didn't even do. Congratulations—you just got played.

See, what he's really sayin' is: *"You gon' beg for my attention. You gon' earn this next phone call. You gon' prove your worth while I sit here and do absolutely nothin'."* And you? You fall into the trap, thinkin' if you just wait long enough, love will come back with a sweet voice and an "I miss you." Nah. What comes back is more silence, maybe a dry-ass message just long enough to keep you hopeful. Then boom—*ghost mode* again.

This ain't love. This is ego-feeding mind control. This is him starvin' you emotionally, so the next crumb he throws feels like a fuckin' feast. And you eat it up, because silence got you feelin' like you ain't shit without him.

But let me be real with you—**you are not the problem**. His silence ain't deep. It ain't spiritual. It's not him "processing" anything. It's a power play. He wants to see how far you'll go just to hear his voice again. That's control, baby. That's narcissism wrapped in quiet. And that shit will *gut your self-worth* if you let it.

So let's get somethin' straight. Stop blaming yourself for a man's decision to go mute. Stop lettin' silence rewrite your story like you broke somethin'. You didn't. He did. And the longer you sit in it, the deeper that wound's gonna cut.

§12.2 – The Mind Game They Never Admit They're Playin'

"He Ain't Taking a Break — He's Takin' the Throne"

You sittin' there thinkin' it's a timeout, a cooling-off period, like this is some relationship halftime show. Nah, sis. This ain't no break. This is a throne. And guess who's sittin' on it? Him. King Manipulator. You? You down on your knees, not worshippin' love, but beggin' for crumbs.

Every second of that silence is calculated. Don't let the stillness fool you. He ain't lost in deep thought. He's up in that bunk watchin' you unravel like it's his personal soap opera. And the worst part? You let it happen because you thought you were fightin' for love. Girl, you ain't fightin' for love — you fightin' for **proof that you're still worth a goddamn reply.**

"This Ain't Love, It's a Fuckin' Setup"

Let's call it what it is. You're sittin' there replaying every damn convo y'all ever had like a crime scene investigator: *"Did I say the wrong thing? Should I have not snapped? Did I push too hard?"* Bitch, stop. You ain't on trial. But he's sure got you actin' like you are. The silence ain't confusion. It's domination. It's about makin' you so desperate for closure, you'll *create your own guilt* just to make sense of it. That's how they win. They don't even gotta say nothin'. You do all the work yourself.

He knows it. That's the play. He ain't trying to fix shit. He wants you twisted up like a damn pretzel, apologizin' for breathin' too loud. That's not love. That's psychological fuckery, and you're sittin' in it thinkin' it's intimacy.

"Quit Chasin' a Motherfucker Who Ain't Lookin' for You"

Here's where the game ends. You stop waitin' for his voice like it's salvation. You stop sendin' them "I miss you" texts. You stop talkin' to the damn void. You. Stop. Chasin'. You think silence is power? Then **take yours back.** Go ghost right the fuck back. Don't pick up that phone when it finally rings two weeks later with his weak-ass *"Hey stranger."* Don't jump to respond when he sends some dry-ass *"Thinking of you."*

Nah. Let that message rot. You don't owe a damn thing to a man who uses silence like a leash. You not his pet. You not his rehab center. And you sure as hell ain't his emotional sponge. Stop soaking up his bullshit just so he can stay dry.

Keisha's Real Talk – Flip the Fuckin' Script

Let me say this loud for the girls in the back still scrolling through old text threads: **you are not the problem.** Stop waitin' for somebody who's only ever showed you how to suffer in silence. He ain't comin' back to love you. He comin' back when he feel like *flexin'* again. Don't let him. Block his ass. Reclaim your peace. And next time he disappears? Tell him to stay gone.

§12.3 – The Illusion That's Been Fuckin' You Up

Stop Lovin' the Man You Built in Your Head

Girl, it's time to face the truth—you ain't in love, you in delusion. You've been sittin' up at night holdin' onto some fake-ass version of him that only exists in your head, built off a few jail calls, some smooth-ass letters, and a fantasy you cooked up outta loneliness and hope.

That version of him—the one who loves hard, protects your heart, and shows up when shit gets real—*he don't fuckin' exist.* What you got is a quiet manipulator who figured out the less he says, the harder you chase. You start blamin' yourself, analyzin' your own damn words, tryin' to fix somethin' he ain't even tryin' to keep. And that right there? That's not love. That's mental slavery dressed up as loyalty.

That "We Gon' Make It" Line Is His Leash

You keep thinkin' y'all gon' make it—*just one more call, just a little more patience, just a lil' more love.* That's the trap, sis. That's the dope he's been servin' straight to your soul. "We gon' make it" is just prison talk for "Keep waitin' while I keep takin'." And you do. You keep feedin' him your time, your money, your whole damn spirit, thinkin' that if you just give enough, he'll turn into the man you prayed for. But that ain't faith, baby—that's fantasy. And he knows it. He throw you crumbs, and you turn 'em into full-course meals just so the dream don't collapse in your face.

Hope Got You Hooked Like a Junkie

What's wild is, deep down, you already know it's fake. You *feel* the disconnect. But you scared to admit it out loud, 'cause sayin' it means everything you gave was for nothin'. So you keep hopin', keep waitin', keep lyin' to yourself like he's comin' back different. But that hope? That shit's poison. It got you twisted, stuck in a loop where you fight for a man who don't even remember what the fuck he said last week. He ain't confused. He's chillin'. Meanwhile, you're losin' sleep, losin' weight, losin' *you*. That's the real cost of holdin' onto a ghost.

Burn the Fantasy So You Can Breathe Again

Let it go. Let that weak-ass dream die. Let the whole illusion burn to the fuckin' ground. He ain't gonna wake up and love you right. He ain't gonna come out the gates talkin' 'bout marriage and healing. He's not gonna suddenly realize you're the one—not 'cause he can't, but because he *don't want to*. He already showed you what you meant to him by what he gave you: *silence*.

And silence don't lie. Stop waitin' for closure from a man who never gave a fuck in the first place. You ain't gotta write one more damn paragraph in a story he already stopped readin'.

Keisha's Real Talk – Kill the Illusion or It'll Kill You

You can't get better while you still beggin' for a reply. You can't move on while you still hopin' his "I miss you" gon' sound different this time. It won't. It's recycled game with a new timestamp. You wanna heal? Burn the damn fantasy. Stop investin' in his potential and start protectin' your fuckin' peace. He's not the one. He never was. And the sooner you bury that lie, the sooner you get your life back.

§12.4 – Reclaiming Yo' Damn Self

Stop Givin' Power to a Ghost

Let's get this part straight—you don't owe shit to nobody who dipped out on you emotionally, spiritually, mentally, or physically. That man went ghost and still got you spinning like a ceiling fan, tryin' to decode silence like it's a damn riddle. Baby, *he ain't sayin' nothin' 'cause he got nothin' for you.* But you? You out here tradin' your peace for maybes, your energy for "I dunno," and your self-worth for silence. Fuck that. He ain't God. He ain't the prize.

He's just a manipulative ass man who realized quiet cuts deeper than words— and you let him wield that shit like a blade. That ends now. You done beggin'. You done waitin'. You done pacin' around your life like you on hold for a nigga that don't even know what real love looks like.

Rebuild from the Rubble, but Build for YOU

You been puttin' your life on pause hopin' he comes around. You skipped out on opportunities, put your glow on standby, shrunk yourself down into someone easy to love—all for a man who couldn't meet you halfway with a full tank and a map. But this next chapter? It's you-only, bitch. You build now for you.

Not for his return, not for his approval, and sure as hell not for the version of him you imagined in your head. You ain't waitin' on closure—you closin' the fuckin' door your damn self. You know how powerful that is? That's real healing. Not the type that needs his sorry ass to co-sign it. But the kind where you stop askin' "why" and start sayin', *"Watch me."*

They Took Enough—Take Yo' Shit Back

Let's do the math. Time wasted? Gone. Tears cried? Dried up. Energy drained? Spent. The only thing left is the part of you he couldn't kill: your ability to *take your fuckin' life back*. That's what this is. This ain't no soft ass "moving on." This is an extraction mission. You comin' for *every part of yourself* he tried to dull down. Your voice? Louder now. Your spirit? Rebuilding. Your standards? Sky high and bulletproof. Ain't no more makin' excuses for red flags. Ain't no more beggin' for clarity. Ain't no more soft landings for emotional terrorists. You see the game now, and you playin' your own.

Keisha's Real Talk – Walk Like You Got the Whole Block Behind You

You know what healed looks like? It's you laughin' again without checkin' your phone. It's you gettin' dressed for you, not wonderin' if he'll like it. It's you sayin' "Nah, I'm good" when he pops up outta nowhere with some weak-ass "I've changed" voicemail. It's not about "gettin' over him." That's small shit. It's about gettin' back *to you*. The real you. The you before the emotional trauma. The you before you turned down your volume just to keep a man comfortable. That bitch? She back. And she's walkin' with her head high, nails done, bills paid, and zero fucks left to spare.

So next time you wonder what to do with all that silence he left you with? **Fill it with your voice. Your power. Your goddamn comeback.**

§12.5 – The Final Cut: When I Stopped Chasin' Devon

It Started With Silence, Not a Goodbye

It didn't start with a fight, or a breakup speech, or even a fuckin' warning. It started with silence. A few hours. Then a day. Then the days stretched like bad gum, and I was still sittin' there tryin' to make excuses for a man who was actively watchin' me unravel. *"Maybe he's busy,"* I told myself. *"Maybe he's going through something."* Nah, bitch—he was goin' through his options. And I was just one of 'em.

I Begged for Crumbs Like They Were Gold

Every missed call hit like a gut punch. I called. I texted. I apologized for shit I didn't even do. I twisted myself up tryin' to be "understanding" while he played mute like his silence was deep and holy. That man wasn't confused. He was fuckin' calculated. And I was the fool waitin' for a signal that never came. His silence wasn't space—it was control. And I was on the leash.

The Game Was Rigged — And I Was the Damn Prize

The longer he stayed quiet, the more I blamed myself. I started shrinkin'. Waterin' myself down. Dullin' my shine just to keep him comfortable. And then it hit me—*this is the game.* And guess what? I was losin' it with both hands tied. Every time I reached out, I gave him more power. Every time I said sorry for nothin', I handed him the steering wheel and told him to crash me.

The Snap Wasn't Soft — It Was Fuckin' Loud

One morning I woke up and said it: **fuck this.** Not in a whispered prayer. In a rage-filled war cry. I stopped callin'. Stopped waitin'. Stopped checkin' my phone like it was a lifeline. I didn't gently reclaim my peace—I snatched that shit back like it owed me rent. I ain't give no warning. I gave a funeral. And the dead man was Devon.

He Came Back Late — I Ain't Answer the Door

And like clockwork, he slithered back. That weak-ass *"Hey stranger"* text. Like we was playin' tag and he just took a long-ass break. But I wasn't that girl anymore. I was done bein' an emotional vending machine—press the right buttons, get love. Nah, bitch. Machine's broken. Outta service. Go beg somewhere else.

Keisha's Real Talk – Bury Him With His Silence

Devon was never the storm. *I was.* I just forgot. I let him shrink me with silence, guilt, and the fantasy of "what if." But now? I remember who the fuck I am. And I ain't chasin' silence ever again. I'm not waiting for closure from a man who never opened up in the first place. You don't need a reply to walk away. You need a spine—and baby, mine's titanium now.

So if you still sittin' there wonderin' if he'll come back...He might. But you won't be there. Because when you finally cut a man like that off? **You don't look back. You walk like you buried the bitch and kept the shovel.**

§12.6 Raven Commentary

"If You Still Think Silence Is Love, You Didn't Read Shit"

Let's get this out the way first—if you made it to the end of Chapter 12 and you're still tellin' yourself *"Maybe he's just not good at communication,"* then congratulations: **you just missed the whole damn point.** That silence he's throwin' at you ain't confusion. It's *control*. It's how he keeps you emotionally starvin' while pretendin' he's "workin' on himself." No, sis. He's workin' on keepin' you on the hook. And you? You're out here playin' emotional detective for a dude who already gave you his answer—**he just didn't say it with words.**

"Silence Is a Weapon — And You're the Target"

You think it's a break. You think he needs time. But what he *actually* needs is for you to break first. He wants you pacin' the room, second-guessin' your worth, rereadin' every message, wonderin' what you did wrong. That's the plan. That's the move. **He disappears so you chase.** And when he finally does say somethin'? It's just enough to reset the cycle and shut you up. This ain't romance. This is a psychological hustle. You ain't bein' loved—you're bein' *trained*.

"Stop Giving Meaning to a Man Who Ain't Saying Shit"

You ever sit there and say, *"If he didn't care, he wouldn't come back"?* Girl. He comes back 'cause he knows you'll be there. That's not love. That's access. He's not returnin' because he loves you—he's returnin' because he *owns you.* Or at least he thinks he does. And every time you answer, you prove him right. So ask yourself: Why the fuck are you treatin' silence like it's a riddle to solve instead of a red flag to walk away from?

"You Can't Heal While You're Still Hoppin' at His Shadow"

Healing don't happen while you're still waitin' on a response. Closure don't come from the same motherfucker who caused the wound. If you keep hangin' on for his version of "I'm sorry," you're gonna be stuck in Chapter 12 while life moves on without you. He ain't comin' back with the answer. He ain't comin' back to fix it. **And even if he does come back? He ain't different.** He's just bored. Or hungry. Or horny. Or all three.

"Take the Hint — and Then Take the Fuckin' Lead"

The silence you're getting? That *is* the answer. Stop pretending it's not. Stop stretchin' your heart to fill in the blanks he leaves behind. If he don't care enough to speak, then you shouldn't care enough to stay. Point blank. He got nothin' to say? Good. You got somewhere else to be. Don't ask for closure—**be the closure.** End the chapter yourself. Loudly. Permanently.

Keisha and Raven's Real Talk – Don't Just Walk Away. Make It Hurt.

You don't owe him shit. Not one more text. Not one more tear. Not one more ounce of yourself tryin' to explain your worth to a grown-ass man who disappears instead of dealin' with his own mess. He don't get to hurt you in silence and then slide back in when it's convenient. When he goes quiet, you go ghost. When he returns, you don't. When he reaches out, **you treat him like the fuckin' stranger he chose to be.**

You want power back? Then stop whisperin'. Stop hopin'. And start actin' like the bitch he *should've* feared losin'.

§12.7 Larry Levine Commentary

Let me guess. You read this chapter, nodded your head, maybe even underlined a few lines like *"Ooh, that's deep,"* then closed the book and went right back to texting that dusty bastard who's been ignoring you for three days straight.

Congratulations. You've Learned Absolutely Nothing

This chapter wasn't written to entertain you. It wasn't therapy. It was a slap. A full-handed, palm-stinging, pride-shattering slap across the face for every woman out there who keeps mistaking silence for mystery and manipulation for meaning.

Let's get one thing straight: **If a man can disappear on you emotionally, he was never yours.**

 He was his own priority—and you were just the emotional support pet he fed scraps to.

Silence Isn't Deep. It's Cheap.

And you bought it. Full price. You gave this man power every time you answered, explained, checked in, waited, forgave, and justified his absence like it was some kind of spiritual journey. It wasn't. He wasn't in monk mode. He wasn't discovering his inner child. **He was just ignoring you. On purpose.**

You Want Healing? Great.

Then here's the first step: **stop lying to yourself.** That man didn't lose his voice

 He didn't lose his phone. He didn't lose his mind.

He lost interest. And he enjoyed watching you scramble to get it back.

You wanna cry? Cry. You wanna scream? Scream. But when you're done? **Block his ass. Burn the fantasy. And never—and I mean NEVER—chase after silence again.**

Because the second you chase a man who disappears, you become the architect of your own rejection. You teach him that disappearing works. And baby, once he learns that trick? He'll keep doin' it. Over and over. Until you're numb.

This chapter was a fire alarm. You can either wake the fuck up or burn in the same story again with a different name. Your call.

— Larry Levine
(*The only motherfucker in this book who ain't scared to say it exactly how it is.*)

CHAPTER THIRTEEN

Your Next Steps

§13.1 – Burn the Blueprint

By Keisha Davis

Let me say this loud so it echo through whatever prison phone line trying to call your ass next: **don't you ever let a man teach you the same lesson twice.** That blueprint? That sob story? That "baby I'm trying" fairy tale? Burn it. Set that shit on fire and watch the ashes float — 'cause if you don't, you gon' keep rebuilding the same damn trap with different paint.

These dudes got the same fuckin' manual. It don't matter the name, the DOC number, or the state they locked up in — **the hustle's identical.** They find your soft spot, crawl in like a parasite, and feed off your guilt, love, and hope like it's commissary.

I ain't here to be poetic. I'm here to slap the last bit of delusion outta your system. If you still out here thinking *"but my situation's different"* — let me stop you right there. **No, it ain't.**

You got used. Played. Tricked. Lied to. That don't make you weak — it makes you **human**. But what you do **after** you see the game? **That's where your power lives.**

Here's the list. Tattoo it on your fuckin' soul:

- **Don't send no more money.** If he need help, tell him apply for indigent aid like everybody else.
- **Don't write no more letters.** You ain't a pen pal, you a whole woman with a life.
- **Don't answer them guilt-trip calls.** Let 'em echo in silence.
- **Don't feel bad for cutting off access.** You ain't oxygen — he'll survive.

- **Don't romanticize pain.** Struggle love ain't noble, it's a goddamn scam.

You are not a fucking rehab center. You are not a rescue shelter for broken potential. You are not the plot twist in some man's prison fantasy. You are the motherfuckin' ending. **You close the book.**

Let him rot in the story he wrote — while you out here writing a whole damn legacy with your name on it. Now take a breath. And light the match. Burn that blueprint — and don't you *ever* rebuild it.

§13.2 – The Final Mirror

By Raven Sinclair

Let me make this plain, baby girl — if you made it this far in the book, then you already know the game. You ain't blind no more. But knowledge without action? That's just recycled pain dressed up like progress.

So I'm gonna hold up the mirror one last time, and I want you to look *dead into it*. Not for him. Not for the pain. For **you.** For that version of you that deserves more than voice notes from a prison phone and late-night letters soaked in manipulation.

Let me break it down like this:

- **If you still feel sorry for him, that's trauma, not love.**
  Guilt is how they keep you on the hook. It ain't loyalty — it's emotional extortion.

- **If you still checking the clock when his call might come through, you're not free yet.**
  That ringtone ain't love, it's the leash.

- **If you still defending him to your friends, your mama, or yourself... baby, he's already won.**
  Because now you ain't just fighting for him — you're fighting *you*.

You don't owe anyone a goddamn explanation for walking away from a lie. You were the storm.

You were the light. You were the entire *damn reason* he survived half the time.

CON GAMES & BROKEN HEARTS

But he made you feel like a convenience. Like a backup plan with a heartbeat.

So here's your last assignment: **Grieve her.** The old you. The one who tolerated it. Cry if you need to. Scream! Burn the letters! Throw out the visitation photos!

But when you're done? **Walk away like a woman who survived the war and ain't lookin' back.** Because you didn't lose him — **you found you.** And from this point on, you don't answer to anybody that can't match that kind of power.

Welcome to your freedom You earned every damn step.

§13.3 – If You Still Stay, Don't Say Nobody Warned You

By Keisha Davis

Aight, here's where I stop sugarcoatin' shit — not that I ever did. But this right here? This for the ones still ridin' the fence. Still makin' excuses. Still waitin' on some jailhouse fairytale to come true like he gon' pop out that gate and sweep you off your feet in some Hollywood-ass prison romance.

Let me be crystal clear, bitch: **If you stay, you're choosing it.** Ain't no confusion no more. You know the rules. You read the damn playbook. You heard the stories. Hell — you read *mine.* So if you still sendin' money, still takin' collect calls, still cancelin' plans for some half-ass phone romance from a man who can't even take a piss without askin' CO permission — then baby, you *want* the pain. And I ain't got no rescue plan for that.

Let Me Spell It Out So Your Heart Can't Play Dumb Later:

- **He ain't misunderstood. He's manipulative.**
- **He ain't "just tryin' to make it." He's usin' you to stay comfortable while you stay broke.**
- **He ain't your soulmate. He's a slick talkin' scammer with limited options.**

And if you still tryin' to flip this book into a justification for why "your situation is different"? **Bitch, please.** You ain't special to him. You're available. You ain't his blessing. You're his resource. You ain't the one. You're the one *for now*.

Now don't get me wrong — you *can* still turn this shit around. Ain't nobody lock your spirit up but you. But if you choose to stay in that cell with him, then don't cry later when your freedom feel like a foreign language.

Don't post no Facebook quotes talkin' 'bout "loyalty got me lookin' stupid" — **We tried to tell you.**

So this the last time I'm sayin' it. **Don't wait on a man who made a home outta prison to give you a future.**

You better pick *you* before you disappear in his shadow. 'Cause one day you gon' wake up and realize you never lived for yourself — you just funded a fantasy for a grown-ass man who played you like an ATM with emotions. **Let that sink in.** Then ask yourself if that's the legacy you wanna live with.

§13.4 – The Last Damn Warning

Written by Larry Levine

Let me say this once, loud as hell for the bitches in the back still making excuses for the dusty-ass inmate draining their accounts and self-esteem — this book wasn't written to comfort your delusion. It was written to murder that motherfucker in cold blood. The fantasy version of him you keep protecting with loyalty he ain't never earned. The fairytale that's cost you sleep, money, dignity, and your damn identity.

Yeah, I said murder. I'm here to kill the fake love story you keep dragging around like a corpse in stilettos. You ain't in a romance — you're in a **hostage situation with emojis.**

This ain't "healing." This ain't "growth." This is *me* dragging you to the mirror and forcing you to admit that you built your whole emotional ecosystem around a broke, locked-up manipulator who mastered the art of long-distance pimping. That's what this is.

Let's keep it all the way gangsta for a second — you knew. You always knew. From the first time he called collect and talked like a pastor who got caught fucking the choir director. From the moment he said, "You're not like the others" but couldn't remember your kid's name two weeks later. From the first time he guilt-tripped you into sending money *then* hit you with the silent treatment like you forgot your place.

You felt it. You ignored it. Now you're broke, bitter, and defending a dude who's probably juggling pen pals like burner phones. And before you say it — yes, I've been there. Done that. Got the overdraft fees and the therapy bills to prove it. So this ain't judgment. This is intervention, bitch. You don't need closure. You need **clarity**. You don't need his apology. You need **your fucking power back.**

Let's be real: He's not a mystery. He's a script.

- *Love bomb. Guilt trip. Sob story. Commissary request.*
- *Promise. Apology. "I'm growing." Same bullshit next week.*

Wash, rinse, block the dumbass, repeat.

You keep calling it love, but if that shit had a label on it, it'd say:

 "Toxic as fuck. Do not swallow. Will destroy your credit, mental health, and faith in humanity."

You want a final warning? **Here's the truth raw and bleeding:**
 If you're still holding on, it's not 'cause he's special — it's 'cause you're scared of who you'll be without the fantasy. And guess what? That fear ain't love. That's trauma bonding with a side of dick withdrawal.

You're the one feeding the beast. You're the one rewriting red flags into love letters.

You're the one paying for a dream with real cash and real pain.

So let me make it simple:

Close the fucking account.
Block the number.
Tell his mama to lose yours too.

Stop rehearsing your heartbreak like it's a damn stage play.
And start acting like you got one life and no more time to waste on a man who's allergic to accountability and addicted to your kindness.

You don't need his closure. You need a new damn chapter. And this time? You don't write him into the story. **You survive. You thrive. You leave his ass exactly where he belongs — in the past and in the system.**

That's the final message. Not stitched on a pillow. Not sung like a ballad.

Just screamed like the truth. Brutal. Bloody. And long overdue.

NOW WAKE THE FUCK UP AND STOP BEING HIS BITCH!

CON GAMES MODULE ONE

Jailhouse Personality Playbook

Now *this* is what the fuck I'm talkin' about—let's crack open the full *Jailhouse Personality Playbook*. These dudes ain't original, they just pick different costumes depending on what kind of woman they tryna manipulate. We're gonna break down **10 common inmate archetypes**, each with their own script, vibe, and manipulation style.

1. The Poet

He writes long-ass letters full of dramatic metaphors, deep-sounding pain, and fake-ass emotional growth. You'll get poems, half-baked philosophy, and talk about "finding himself." But it's all surface-level. His whole game is making you believe he's emotionally evolved. In reality? He just knows women fall for men who *seem* deep. So he uses pretty words to hide the fact he ain't doing shit to change. You're his emotional fan club, not his partner.

2. The Gangster

He talks hard like he runs the yard—but softens just enough to call you "queen" and make you feel chosen. He wants to sound dangerous and desirable. He'll throw in prison war stories, code language, and flex about who fears him. But under all that tough talk, he's still running game. He uses his "realness" to distract from the fact that he's emotionally unavailable, controlling, and probably juggling three other "queens" on the side.

3. The Preacher

He's found God—or so he says. Every letter starts with scripture, and every phone call is a sermon about redemption. He's playing the righteous man, trying to hook you with spiritual guilt. He'll talk about how you're a blessing, how God sent you, how he's trying to be a better man. But pay attention—he'll still ask for money, still lie, and still manipulate... just with a Bible verse slapped on top. God didn't send you to struggle. He did.

4. The Victim

Every conversation is a sob story. Nothing is ever his fault. The system wronged him. His family turned on him. The guards hate him. His celly's shady. He paints himself as the misunderstood soul just trying to survive. He wants you to feel sorry for him—because pity opens wallets. You'll feel like you need to rescue him, defend him, *fix him*. But guess what? He's not helpless. He's just lazy—and emotional manipulation is his hustle.

5. The Player

He flirts like it's a damn art form. Smooth voice, sexy words, late-night fantasy talk. He calls you "baby girl" and makes you feel like you're the baddest thing alive. You'll feel desired, pursued, seen—but it's all smoke. This dude's playing the field, keeping his options open, and making every woman feel like she's the one. You're in a rotation, sweetheart. His game is attention, not commitment—and he knows exactly how to keep you hooked.

6. The Intellectual

This one hits you with big words and big ideas. He reads Nietzsche now, writes essays about society, and acts like prison made him smarter than the rest of us. He's condescending with a touch of charm. His whole hustle is impressing you with intelligence so you overlook his bullshit. He'll debate you, correct you, and "educate" you—but won't ever *own up* to his own patterns. Deep down, he ain't seeking a partner. He wants a student.

7. The Daddy

This one plays protector from a distance. "You mine." "Ain't nobody touchin' what's mine." He calls you "baby," "girl," "my lil one." Makes you feel safe, chosen, claimed. But it's control masked as care. He starts checking who you talk to, what you wear, how you post. He builds emotional walls around you while still feeding off your support. You feel wanted—but what you really are is *owned*. He ain't your daddy. He's your warden.

8. The Artist

He sends sketches, tattoos, love letters, and handmade gifts. He taps into your nurturing side, like "look how talented and gentle I am." He creates this image of himself as a tortured creative just trying to make it. It feels authentic. But check his pattern—he's using charm, talent, and effort to earn your sympathy, your validation, and eventually, your wallet. This dude paints pictures so you'll ignore the truth: *he's just painting you a fantasy*.

9. The Reformer

This one claims he's all about "the cause." Prison politics, injustice, the youth, reform—he's speaking that woke shit. He wants to seem like he's *bigger than his past*. Talks activism, quotes Malcolm X, maybe even writes a book or two. But watch how he uses it: he manipulates your values. If you challenge him, he hits you with "you just don't get it." He's not looking for a partner—he's looking for a cheerleader to fund his revolution *and* his commissary.

10. The Ghost

Silent type. Mysterious. Never says too much. But when he *does* open up, it hits hard. He makes you crave those moments, like you're earning his trust one tear at a time. But it's all calculated. He's mastered silence as a power move. You do all the emotional lifting while he keeps his cards close. It keeps you addicted—always wondering, always chasing more. He's not deep. He's *just not available*. You're building the whole bond in your head.

There it is. Ten fake-ass flavors of the same manipulation sundae. He might be a poet, a preacher, or a player—but trust me: **if he's locked up and you're doing all the emotional, financial, and mental labor? You're being played.**

Let me know if you want these in a chart, infographic, or part of a chapter breakdown. I'll dress it up or strip it down however you want.

CON GAMES MODULE TWO

Inmate Breakup Scripts

You want out? Good. I got the damn scissors, and I ain't just cuttin' the cord—I'm severin' it with a machete. This section right here? It's for when you're DONE. No long explanations. No back-and-forth. No room for him to talk you into circles.

This is "Breakup Scripts"—word-for-word lines you can drop, send, or speak that shut it down and lock it down. After this? Block. Delete. Breathe. Reclaim your peace.

1. The Cold Exit (Text Version)

"This is the last message you'll get from me. I'm done with the lies, the guilt, the money drains, and the manipulation. I gave you my time, my heart, and more than you earned. Now I'm giving myself peace. Don't respond. I won't read it. Goodbye."

Use when you want zero drama. Burn the bridge and block the number right after.

2. The No-Nonsense Call-Off

"You used me. Whether you meant to or not doesn't matter anymore. I'm not your bank, your therapist, or your punching bag. I'm done. Don't call me again. I won't be picking up."

Use this one if he's on the phone. Then hang up mid-sentence if he tries to argue.

3. The Power Pivot

"I'm choosing me now. That means no more letters, no more calls, no more holding it down for someone who ain't holding me up. Lose this number and figure your own shit out."

For when you wanna remind him you're not weak—you're walking strong.

4. The Receipt Returner

"I counted up every dollar, every excuse, every broken promise—and the math don't lie. I paid for my own heartbreak. But I'm done financing it. Don't contact me again."

Savage. Send it, then screenshot it—for your healing, not his response.

5. The Godspeed Goodbye (for the spiritual types)

"I wish you peace in your life, but I no longer want to be a part of it. I deserve honesty, growth, and freedom—not games. God bless. Goodbye."

Use when you want to stay calm, spiritual, and still walk the fuck away.

6. The Emotional Cutoff

"Whatever I felt for you is gone. I cried, I doubted, I bent over backwards—and all I got was empty promises. You don't deserve another second of me. This is closure. Don't respond."

Best sent after one too many letdowns. Period. No tears left.

7. The Blunt Bitch Exit

"I ain't your momma, your maid, or your damn commissary fairy. You got three other bitches runnin' the same script, and I'm not about to be one of 'em. Blocked. Bye."

For when you've had ENOUGH and want to exit loud and clear.

8. The Accountability Demand

"You lied. You manipulated. You took and never gave. Don't ever confuse my silence for forgiveness. I'm not bitter. I'm just better—without you."

Hits him in the ego. That's where the truth hurts most.

9. The Ghost Mode Trigger

"We're done. You'll never hear from me again. No warning, no second chances, no explanation. Just silence. Watch me disappear."

Use when you want to go full Casper the unfuckwithable ghost.

10. The I've Evolved Exit

"The woman you used to talk to? She don't live here anymore. She grew up, woke up, and walked out. And she ain't lookin' back."

Say this one with your chest. Then go pour a drink and celebrate you.

Keisha:

Girl, pick the one that fits your fire. Copy. Paste. Send.
Then BLOCK his ass like your peace depends on it—'cause it does.
Need help turning this into a full printable "exit kit"? I got more smoke where that came from.

CON GAMES MODULE THREE

Messages Proving He's Playing You

(AKA: If he says this, your heart ain't the only thing he's hustlin'.)

1. "You the only one who ever really held me down."

Translation: "You're the one sendin' the most money right now."

Why it's manipulation: It's vague, sweet, and makes you feel special. But he's copy-pasting this line to every chick with a working debit card.

2. "I ain't askin' for nothin', I just need you to understand I'm struggling."

Translation: "I *am* asking for something, but I want you to *offer* so I don't look like a user."

Why it's manipulation: He's using reverse psychology to guilt you into offering help. Don't fall for it.

3. "You mad? I guess you don't love me like I love you."

Translation: "I'm flipping the blame so you feel guilty for reacting to *my* bullshit."

Why it's manipulation: Classic gaslighting. You become the villain just for setting boundaries.

4. "If you really loved me, you'd do this one thing for me."

Translation: "Let me see how far I can push you under the name of 'love.'"

Why it's manipulation: Conditional love ain't love. It's emotional blackmail in a hoodie.

5. "When I get out, we gon' build something real. I promise."

Translation: "Stay loyal, keep sending shit, and don't notice I'm not doing anything to actually deserve you."

Why it's manipulation: The future fantasy game. No action, just empty promises to keep you stuck.

6. "These other chicks just don't get me like you do."

Translation: "You're my current favorite. For now."

Why it's manipulation: He's triangulating. You feel like the chosen one when really you're just winning the game—for now.

7. "Damn, I thought you was different."

Translation: "You didn't fall for my shit today, and I don't like that."

Why it's manipulation: He's testing your need to prove you're "better" than his ex or other women. It's bait.

8. "You don't know what it's like in here."

Translation: "I'm about to excuse anything I say or do behind the 'I'm locked up' card."

Why it's manipulation: He's shifting the focus from his actions to your guilt. It shuts down your right to question him.

9. "I ain't got nobody else but you."

Translation: "Don't go nowhere—I need your support, money, and emotional labor."

Why it's manipulation: Isolation tactic. Makes you feel like abandoning him is heartless, even when he's draining the hell outta you.

10. "You actin' different lately... who you talkin' to?"

Translation: "I feel you slippin' away and I'm tryin' to reel you back in with paranoia."

Why it's manipulation: Possessiveness dressed as concern. He's flipping insecurity into control.

Girl, print this shit out. Tape it to your wall. Keep it in your damn purse. Because the moment he hits you with one of these lines, you'll know—it ain't love, it's strategy.

CON GAMES MODULE FOUR

Fictional Scam Letters From Inmates

Read these like your bank account depends on it. Because it might!!!

Welcome to *Module Four*, where we dive deep into the heart of the manipulation machine: the written word. These aren't just love letters. They're **weapons**, dressed in romance, dipped in guilt, and stamped with a return address from behind the wall.

What you're about to read are fictional letters—but don't let that word fool you. Every single one is based on **real tactics, real wording, and real emotional traps** used by inmates to scam, seduce, and emotionally hijack women on the outside. These letters are ripped straight from the psychological playbook of prison hustlers—each one crafted to mirror a specific archetype:

The Poet

The Preacher

The Gangster

The Victim

The Player

The "Daddy"

And the Ghost

Each letter is followed by **a full breakdown by Keisha Davis**, who exposes the tactics, flips the emotional script, and calls out every manipulative move like she's dissecting a crime scene. You're not just reading these for entertainment—you're learning how the game is played.

How to Read This Module:

Don't get caught up in the emotions. These letters are designed to make you feel seen, needed, and "different." That's the trap.

Pay attention to the patterns. There's always a formula: flattery → pain → guilt → money ask → future faking → reassurance.

Use Keisha's commentary like armor. After every letter, she tears the manipulation apart so you can *see it for what it is*, not what you want it to be.

Ask yourself the hard questions. If any of these letters feel familiar, it's time to stop romanticizing and start protecting yourself.

This chapter isn't here to entertain—it's here to **wake your ass up**. These are the emotional blueprints of con games that destroy lives, drain wallets, and leave women blaming themselves for believing lies that were custom-designed to fool them.

Read carefully. Learn fast. And if you're already getting letters like this? **Read slower.** Because your freedom might be on the line—even if you're not the one doing the time

Fictional Letter #1: "The Poet's Lure

From: Darnell J. (#5780034)
Location: Cellblock C, Unit 3B
Date: September 17

My Queen,

It's crazy how someone can be trapped behind four concrete walls, surrounded by chaos, and still feel peace... just by thinking about you. That's what you give me—peace in a place built to break men down. Ain't no one out here real like that.

When I close my eyes, I see you. Not just your beauty, but your energy, your heart, your presence. It's like you've been the missing piece to my soul this whole time, and God just waited 'til now to send you. Maybe that's why this pain happened. Maybe He locked me up so I could finally find something real.

I ain't gonna front—these last few days been heavy. Dudes actin' shady, drama poppin' off, people turnin' cold on me like I ain't never been solid for them. But you? You never switched. You stayed consistent, even when I know it's been hard for you too. That means everything to me.

Real talk—I ain't had someone ride for me like you. Not even my own blood. People always got excuses. "I got bills." "I got kids." But when I hear your voice, when I read your words... I feel like I still matter. Like I ain't just another number in the system.

And that's what makes this hard to say.

You know I don't like askin' for shit. That's not who I am. But right now... I'm strugglin'. Not just mentally, but for real—for basics. I'm outta soap. I ain't eaten nothin' but state trays for a week. I got cats out here gettin' packages and livin' good off women who don't even love them. Meanwhile, the one woman I love? I'm scared to ask her for help because I don't want her to think that's all I care about.

But I gotta be honest—if there's any way you could bless me with like $40 or $50 on JPay, just to grab some hygiene and maybe a few soups? That'd help me breathe. That don't make me weak. It makes me real. I'm asking the only person who's ever seen me for a little support—not because you owe me, but because you've always been the only one who gave a damn without keepin' score.

You told me you were tired the other night. You didn't say much on the phone. And I felt that. You been holdin' me down, and I know it's taken a toll. I don't want to be the reason you feel drained. I want to be the man that builds you up, even from in here.

That's why I been writin' every day. I got that poem comin' for you, too. Been workin' on it in my bunk at night. Just know I ain't never stop thinkin' about us. I still got that plan in my head—me and you, gettin' a spot together, startin' fresh. I want kids. I want late-night talks. I want to be the man who gives you the world you always gave to everyone else but never got in return.

Don't let this place make you doubt me. I know you hear stories. I know people tell you these dudes run game. But I'm not them. I'm him. I'm the one that's gonna prove this love ain't just phone calls and letters—it's legacy. It's purpose.

But I can't build if I'm breakin'.

So if you can, send what you can. And if you can't, just write me. That's all I ask. Just don't leave me in this darkness. Don't let this system win by takin' the one light I got left.

You already saved me once. Let me hold onto that.

All my love, always—
Darnell

Kiesha's Reflections on Darnell

Alright ladies, let me break this bullshit down like I'm teaching a class called Manipulation 101: Inmate Edition. That letter from Darnell? Yeah—it's a weapon, not a love letter. It's the kind of scam so smooth you'll swear it's sincerity... until you wake up broke, used, and emotionally wrecked.

Here's the exact anatomy of the scam in that letter:

1. Emotional Hook (Lines 1–3)

"When I close my eyes, I see you... You give me peace... God sent you to me..."

What he's doing:
He opens with flattery, soul talk, and spiritual destiny bullshit to create an instant emotional high. He paints you as the answer to his pain, which hooks nurturing women who crave purpose or want to be seen as "different."

Scam move: This ain't about you—it's about setting you up to carry his emotional weight. Once you feel special, you'll ignore the red flags.

2. Victim Vibes (Mid-paragraph)

"People turning cold on me... No one rides for me like you..."

What he's doing:
He paints himself as the abandoned underdog. Everyone's left him—except you. That creates a savior complex. Now you feel obligated to stick around, even if your gut says something's off.

Scam move: Isolation tactic. Makes you feel like his whole survival depends on you. It's psychological blackmail.

3. Financial Softball (Guilt-Twist Request)

"I hate asking, but... just $40 to get some food and hygiene..."

What he's doing:
Here comes the real reason for the letter—money. But notice how he wraps it in shame and reluctance. That's to lower your guard. "I hate asking" = I've mastered how to ask without sounding like I'm using you.

Scam move: He's manipulating you into offering support so he don't look like a leech—while still taking your cash.

4. Future Fable Setup

"I still got that plan in my head... kids, late-night talks, starting fresh..."

What he's doing:
He paints the dream. A fantasy life with you outside those walls. This creates false hope and makes the investment feel "worth it." The more you imagine that future, the more likely you'll tolerate the present.

Scam move: Classic bait-and-dangle. Keeps you emotionally locked in while he enjoys the benefits right now.

5. Defensive Preemptive Strike

"I know people tell you these dudes run game... but I'm not them."

What he's doing:
He knows you've heard stories about prison hustles, so he disarms it ahead of time. That's a power move—he's flipping suspicion into reassurance before you can even raise the question.

Scam move: "I'm not like the others" is exactly what they all say. It's the gas station of lies—cheap, everywhere, and always open.

6. Re-Shaming & Re-Hooking Close

"If you can't send money, just write... just don't leave me in this darkness..."

What he's doing:
This is the closer. He's making it seem like your emotional support alone is enough... but not really. If you don't help, the guilt still lands. Now you're the one who'd be abandoning him.

Scam move: Even if you don't send cash, you stay emotionally connected—making you easier to hit up again next week.

The Full Picture:

He opened with flattery.

Shifted into emotional dependency.

Slid in a guilt-wrapped request.

Promised a future that doesn't exist.

Deflected suspicion with fake vulnerability.

Closed with just enough shame to keep you close even if you say no.

This is weaponized romance.
It's not sloppy—it's choreographed. He's runnin' this same script on three other women, each customized by their weaknesses.

Kiesha's Final Reflections on Darell

So yeah, Darnell ain't just writing love letters—he's running a miniature emotional Ponzi scheme. You keep investing, hoping that "one day" will come, but the return on investment is always negative.

Fictional Letter #2: "The Preacher's Play"

From: Elijah M. (#1138821)
Location: Faith Dorm, C-Pod
Date: October 3

Peace and Grace to You, My Angel,

I pray this letter finds you in good health and even better spirit. I just came from the chapel, and while I sat there in reflection, your name kept rising in my heart. The Lord's been talking to me about you lately. About your purpose. Your strength. The role you've been called to play—not just in my life, but in the bigger picture of redemption and restoration.

I truly believe God doesn't make mistakes. He didn't send you into my life by chance. He positioned you to walk with me through this valley. You're not just a blessing—you're assignment. And baby, I take that seriously.

Every day in here is a spiritual battle. Temptation. Darkness. Weak-minded men who gave up on hope. But I keep fighting, because I've got someone like you on the outside reminding me what's waiting beyond these walls. I know you get tired. I know the enemy whispers lies to make you question what we have. But let me tell you something—the devil don't attack what ain't divine. That's why this gets hard. That's why you feel tested.

Because this? Us? It's sacred.

I spent this morning fasting and asking God for guidance. I asked Him to protect you, to keep your heart full even when your hands are empty. And I also asked Him to open a door—for support, for provision, for survival. Because truthfully, things in here have been tough lately.

I wouldn't bring this to you unless I was led to. But the unit store opened this week, and I've got nothing on my books. I need hygiene, some food, even just a stamp or two so I can keep ministering to the younger brothers in here who ain't got no one. I'm not asking you—I'm trusting God to move through you. If it's on your heart to help, I'll be grateful. If it ain't, I'll still be praying for you all the same.

This isn't about money—it's about ministry. About purpose. About obedience to the Spirit. I know you're faithful. I know your heart. And I believe you'll be rewarded for your sacrifice. Don't let anyone tell you otherwise.

I'm keeping the vision. I still see our home. Our Sundays together. You in the kitchen, me in my Bible, us raising kids that know love, not survival. This world tried to break us, but God? He builds with broken pieces.

Write me soon. I need your light in here. And if it's on your heart to send anything, I'll receive it in faith.

With love,
In Christ,
Elijah

Kiesha's Reflections on Elijah

Aight, I'm about to rip the mask off this holy hustle and show you the scam underneath all that preachy sugar talk. Elijah's letter ain't about faith—it's about finesse. He's not leading a flock; he's leading a **financial revival with your bank account as the offering plate**. Let's dissect this smooth-talking, Bible-wrapped con job **line by line**.

1. Divine Assignment Setup

"You're not just a blessing—you're an assignment."
What he's doing:
He's elevating her from a supportive woman to a spiritually obligated servant. Now she's not just loving him—she's carrying out God's will. That's psychological handcuffs dressed in gold leaf.

Scam move: He rewires her role from "girlfriend" to "God-sent." If she backs out now, she's not rejecting a man—she's disobeying the Creator.

2. Faith-Based Victim Card

"Every day in here is a spiritual battle... I keep fighting because I've got someone like you..."
What he's doing:
He's linking his survival to her support—emotionally and spiritually. He makes her feel like his faith, sanity, and transformation depend on her staying in his life.

Scam move: It's a burden disguised as a compliment. He shifts his survival onto her shoulders so she can't walk away without guilt.

3. Doubt-Shaming by Devil Talk

"The devil don't attack what ain't divine."
What he's doing:
He's reframing her doubts. Instead of listening to her intuition, he tells her those red flags are actually "attacks" on their holy union.

Scam move: Gaslighting cloaked in gospel. He makes her distrust herself and trust him more, no matter how shady he acts.

4. The Fasting and Praying Warm-Up

"I spent this morning fasting and asking God for guidance…"
What he's doing:
He preps her for the money ask by saying it came straight from a spiritual ritual. So now it's not his request—it's divine instruction.

Scam move: Spiritual manipulation at its slickest. He removes personal accountability and makes her think God cosigned the hustle.

5. Financial Softball (Guilt-Twist Request)

"I'm not asking you—I'm trusting God to move through you…"
What he's doing:
This is the money ask—but wrapped in holy language to make it feel sacred, not selfish. He don't want to ask—he wants her to feel called to give.

Scam move: He turns her wallet into a spiritual weapon. She's not giving to a man—she's "obeying God." If she resists, it ain't about boundaries, it's a crisis of faith.

6. Reframing the Hustle

"This isn't about money—it's about ministry."
What he's doing:
He takes a basic ask for hygiene and food and flips it into a righteous cause. Now it's a mission, not a favor.

Scam move: This is the rebrand. He knows it's begging—but rebrands it as service so she'll give more and feel good about it.

7. Future Fantasy Investment

"I still see our home... You in the kitchen, me in my Bible..."
What he's doing:
He's dangling a soft, peaceful dream of life together to keep her emotionally hooked. It makes her sacrifice feel like she's building toward something.

Scam move: Future-faking. He sells the fantasy to keep her loyal, obedient, and generous in the present. She's investing in a life that ain't coming.

8. Passive Guilt Exit

"If it's on your heart to send anything, I'll receive it in faith."
What he's doing:
He ends soft, as if he's not pressuring her—but the emotional weight is real. He puts the decision on her conscience.

Scam move: This ain't kindness—it's manipulation with a gentle tone. He makes her feel like not helping means her heart isn't right.

Kiesha's Final Reflections on Elijah

So there it is—eight layers deep of pure prison-polished manipulation. It's not loud, it's lethal. Because he ain't scamming from a cell, he's scamming from the pulpit he built in your emotions. Let's line up the next letter when you're ready. The Gangster? The Player? The Victim? Pick your poison.

Fictional Letter #3: "The Gangster's Grip"

From: Marquis D. (#8893201)
Location: Block 4A, Max Unit
Date: October 14

What's good, Ma,

I'm gonna keep it a hundred—my head been heavy lately. Shit's been wild in here. Politics got the tier tense. Muthafuckas actin' shady. I can't trust nobody but you. You my calm. You my real. I look at your pictures, and it's like everything slow down for a minute. I don't give a fuck what they say—I know you was made for me.

That's why I get tight when I feel you slippin'. Don't act like I don't notice. You used to write me like clockwork. Now I'm sittin' here wonderin' if some clown out there got your time. You out there laughin' while I'm in here battlin' demons? That ain't loyalty, baby.

But I ain't gonna come at you sideways. I'm just lettin' you know—if we locked in, then we locked all the way in. Ain't no half-steppin'. I call you mine, and I mean that with my whole chest. You wearin' my name every time you pick up that phone.

I need you to remember who the fuck I am. I'm a man that moves with power, with pride. I don't beg. But I do expect my queen to hold shit down. And right now? Commissary dropped, and I ain't got nothin' to my name. No hygiene, no food, no nothin'. My people flaked. So yeah, I need you to slide me somethin'. Fifty would be love. More if you can swing it.

I ain't with the games. I don't do lies. You say you love me? Prove it. This ain't no test—it's real life. I'm on lockdown, and I still protect you with my spirit. Who you think prays for you when you sleepin'? Who got you on they mind while they dodgin' bullshit in here?

I know you tired. I know the world pullin' at you. But I need you to tighten up. You ain't out there single. You got a man. One who's countin' on you to stay solid. That's what I need right now—solid.

Write me back quick. Don't leave me guessin'. That's how people get replaced.

Your King,
Marq

Kiesha's Reflections on Marq

Aight, let's break down **Marq's manipulative masterpiece**—because that letter wasn't love, baby. That was **a psychological headlock with a kiss on the forehead**. This dude ain't just pushing buttons—he built a whole control panel. I'mma rip it apart line by line so you see how he flips **power, guilt, and loyalty** into a trap.

1. Thugged-Out Emotional Hook

"Politics got the tier tense... I can't trust nobody but you."
What he's doing:
He sets the scene: chaos, danger, betrayal. Then slides her in as his only source of peace. It flatters her, puts pressure on her, and isolates her into a savior role.

Scam move: Classic isolation tactic. If she's "all he's got," then walking away feels like abandonment—even if she's being drained.

2. Loyalty Check with Guilt Blade

"Don't act like I don't notice... That ain't loyalty, baby."
What he's doing:
This is passive-aggressive pressure. He's accusing her of emotional cheating for not writing on time—dropping guilt without proof.

Scam move: It forces her to explain herself, defend herself, and reprove her loyalty—giving him more control.

3. Ownership Through Language

"I call you mine... You wearin' my name every time you pick up that phone."
What he's doing:
He's not being romantic—he's marking territory. He's reminding her she's not independent. She's his. Always.

Scam move: Dominance disguised as devotion. Creates an illusion of deep love, but it's just possessiveness with prison poetry.

4. The Financial Ultimatum

"I don't beg. But I do expect my queen to hold shit down... Slide me somethin'. Fifty would be love."
What he's doing:
Here comes the real reason for the letter: money. He claims pride to avoid looking needy, then demands help as an expectation of love.

Scam move: It's a flex wrapped around a financial leash. "I don't beg" is smoke—he's manipulating her into proving love with cash.

5. Emotional Blackmail

"You say you love me? Prove it."
What he's doing:
He weaponizes her feelings. Love isn't a feeling to him—it's a transaction. And he's demanding payment.

Scam move: This is **straight-up blackmail** with a romantic mask. It ties her value to what she gives, not who she is.

6. Spiritual Control Add-On

"Who got you on they mind while they dodgin' bullshit in here?"
What he's doing:
He paints himself as a warrior fighting for her—even from behind bars. He invokes protection, prayer, and sacrifice to guilt her into giving more.

Scam move: It's fake sacrifice to justify real control. He ain't fighting for her—he's fighting to keep his hustle flowing.

7. Identity Control

"You ain't out there single. You got a man."
What he's doing:
He's redefining her identity without her permission. She don't get to move how she wants—she's his, period.

Scam move: This is the cornerstone of **jailhouse emotional control**. He strips away her independence and uses the label to justify expectations.

8. Subtle Threat Closer

"Write me back quick. Don't leave me guessin'. That's how people get replaced."
What he's doing:
There it is—the quiet threat. Don't delay. Don't pull back. Don't fuck around. Or you'll be swapped out like expired milk.

Scam move: Coercion wrapped in charm. Keeps her scared of losing him, when really, she should be running.

Kiesha's Final Reflections on Marq

This ain't love. It's **possession**, **control**, and **financial extortion** dressed up in street loyalty and poetic threats.nHe's running game by using just enough sweet to coat the poison. But it's still poison, girl.

Fictional Letter #4: "The Victim's Violin"

From: Terrance L. (#7741906)
Location: Med Unit, Tier 2 East
Date: October 28

Hey...

I didn't even know if I should write you. I been sitting on this for a minute. Honestly? I feel like I'm losin' you. And maybe that's my fault. Maybe I pushed you too hard. Maybe I expected too much. But that's all I ever do—expect too much from people who leave.

That's my story. That's always been my story.

I ain't slept right in weeks. My appetite gone. I'm back on meds. I feel like I'm drowning in a place where no one even notices when you stop breathing. But I always thought you did. I always thought you could feel me from out there. That's why this distance hurts so bad.

I know you're busy. I know life ain't easy. But when days go by and I don't hear from you, it fucks me up. It's like everything good I thought I had slips away, and I'm right back in that dark place where I ain't worth shit to nobody. I know I ain't perfect. I know I made mistakes. But dammit, don't I deserve one person who won't throw me away?

You told me you'd be there. You told me I wasn't alone. But I feel more alone now than I ever did before you came into my life. I trusted you with my pain. With my truth. And now? I'm scared to even ask you how you feel. Scared you'll say what I already know. That you're done.

And I get it. You ain't obligated to deal with me. I'm just some guy behind a wall, right? I'm the fuckup. The inmate. The problem. But you made me believe I was more than that. You made me believe I could be more than that.

I'm trying to hold on. But I'm tired. And broke. And my meds run out next week. The nurse said I gotta pay for refills now. I hate even bringing that up, but it's real. If you can help… just anything… it might give me enough strength to keep trying.

But if you can't… just don't leave me without saying goodbye. I been abandoned enough in my life. I couldn't take that from you too.

Still hoping,
T

Kiesha's Reflections on Terrance

Oh, you already know I'm about to tear this guilt-drenched sob story into shreds. Terrance ain't writin' no letter—he's composing a goddamn emotional trap in slow motion. Every line is designed to make you question your own boundaries, feel bad for breathing without him, and open your damn wallet out of pity.

Let's dissect this **manipulative masterpiece**.

1. Opening With Hesitation

"I didn't even know if I should write you."
What he's doing:
Instant vulnerability. Makes her feel like she's in control. But really, he's laying

groundwork for guilt. "I almost didn't write" is code for you're hurting me, but I'm too broken to say it direct.

Scam move: Opens soft so he can set up the emotional punch. It disarms her into listening longer, even if she was ready to block his ass.

2. Abandonment Setup

"That's my story. That's always been my story."
What he's doing:
He's painting himself as the lifelong victim. He wants her to feel like she's part of a tragic pattern—like if she leaves, she's just like the rest.

Scam move: It's guilt-wrapped pressure. He don't say "Don't leave"—he makes leaving feel like emotional murder.

3. Health Crisis Bait

"I ain't slept... I'm back on meds..."
What he's doing:
Now he brings in the emotional and physical pain. He's not just sad—he's deteriorating. Her silence is literally making him sick.

Scam move: This is full-on **sympathy extortion**. She's not just a girlfriend now—she's being guilted into acting like a caretaker.

4. Playing the Invisible Card

"No one even notices when you stop breathing..."
What he's doing:
He elevates her role. Out of a whole damn prison system, she's the only one who cares. It makes her feel special—but also completely responsible for his survival.

Scam move: He makes her the sole lifeline. That's emotional blackmail in a love letter.

5. Guilt Through Absence

"When days go by and I don't hear from you, it fucks me up."
What he's doing:

He's framing her silence as a direct cause of his emotional collapse. Now she can't even take a break without being blamed.

Scam move: He's tying her presence to his stability. If she distances herself, she's now the reason he's spiraling.

6. Fragile Male Ego Dressed as Heartbreak

"Don't I deserve one person who won't throw me away?"
What he's doing:
He don't ask if she's tired. He shames her into staying. The minute she pulls back, he plays the "everybody gives up on me" card.

Scam move: It's emotional entrapment. He makes her fear becoming his next trauma.

7. Emotional Restraint as Manipulation

"I'm scared to even ask you how you feel."
What he's doing:
He pretends to protect her feelings, but really he's forcing her to speak up—so she has to reassure him.

Scam move: This ain't modesty—it's a trap. It pressures her to confess loyalty to ease his pretend insecurity.

8. The Underdog Monologue

"I'm just some guy behind a wall, right?"
What he's doing:
He's degrading himself just enough to activate her need to prove she doesn't see him that way. He wants her to chase the idea that she's different.

Scam move: Pity-fishing. He insults himself so she'll defend him and try to "show" she cares—usually with money.

9. Financial Softball (Guilt-Twist Request)

"My meds run out next week... If you can help... it might give me enough strength to keep trying."

What he's doing:

Boom. Here's the real reason for the letter. But he don't ask. He frames it as a survival need, tacked on at the end like a whisper.

Scam move: Classic bait-and-bleed. Emotional collapse first, financial squeeze last. And he attaches the money to his will to keep living. That's next-level emotional extortion.

10. Closing With Guilt and Fear

"Just don't leave me without saying goodbye..."
What he's doing:

He paints abandonment as psychological trauma. He don't beg her to stay—he dares her to walk away and live with the guilt.

Scam move: This ain't a goodbye plea. It's a trapdoor. If she leaves, she becomes the villain in his sad-ass story.

Kiesha's Final Reflections on Terrance

Terrance is the master of the **slow-burn sob story**. He don't yell. He don't demand. He bleeds all over her inbox and makes her feel like **she's responsible for cleaning it up**. He ain't in love. He's in survival mode—and you're the life raft he'll drag under just to keep himself afloat.

Fictional Letter #5: "The Player's Fantasy"

From: Andre L. (#6621984)
Location: C-Yard, Bldg 6, Lower Tier
Date: November 4

Hey sexy,

Damn, I don't even know how to start this letter without smilin'. I was just layin' here thinkin' about you—about that laugh, that lil look you give when you tryna act like you ain't blushing. You got me stuck, girl. Straight up.

I ain't gon' lie—when I first wrote you, I thought it'd just be somethin' casual. You know, a lil escape from all this madness in here. But you? You flipped that whole plan. You got me feelin' shit I forgot was even real. I don't talk to nobody else the way I talk to you. You different. You real.

You ever think about what we'd be like if I was out? I do. All the time. I picture us laid up in a hotel somewhere—you in one of them little tank tops and no panties, sittin' on the edge of the bed smilin' while I roll up. Music low. Lights dim. And I'm behind you, whisperin' in your ear, askin' what you want next. And you say... "Everything."

That's what I wanna give you. Everything.

But that's future talk. Right now? I just need you to keep holdin' me down while I get through this shit. You the one thing that makes this time bearable. Ain't no fake vibes with you. You got that raw energy. That natural sexy. I swear, even on my worst days, just thinkin' about you makes me smile like I ain't locked behind no fuckin' steel door.

Look, I ain't tryna make this about money, but my books look like a damn desert right now. I'm down to one soap and half a deodorant. Real talk, I feel like I smell myself. If you could bless me with somethin'—even $40—I'd be able to get right and keep my head straight. I know you don't owe me nothin', and I ain't the type to stress you. Just sayin', if you can, I'd appreciate it like crazy.

You my light, ma. You my motivation. I can't wait for the day I slide my hands down your thighs and say, "Now it's my turn to take care of you."

Until then? Keep that sexy ass smile on. And don't forget—I'm thinkin' about you harder than you'll ever know.

Yours for real,
Dre

Kiesha's Reflections on Dre

That letter right there? Whew. It's damn near erotic fiction with a side of psychological theft. It's flirtation, future-fakin', and financial hustling wrapped in damn, he fine energy.

Want me to break it down next? I'll tear that shit apart and show you every move that makes it a high-gloss scam. Let's go.

Oh you already KNOW I'm about to rip this smooth-talking motherfucker wide open. Andre's letter is sexy, slick, and soaked in fantasy—but underneath that charm? **It's a damn con job with cologne on it.** Every word is a carefully planned play, and he's selling dreams to **cover the price tag.** Let's dissect the **Player's Playbook** piece by piece.

1. Flirty Emotional Hook

"Damn, I don't even know how to start this letter without smilin'…"
What he's doing:
He comes in soft, warm, and personal—starting off like this is just another daydream between lovers. He's building a comfort bubble so she lets her guard down.

Scam move: He's framing the letter as a feel-good escape, so when the hustle hits later, it doesn't feel like a transaction—it feels like intimacy.

2. Rewriting the Origin Story

"When I first wrote you… I thought it'd just be somethin' casual."
What he's doing:
He's pretending she turned him from a player into a believer. That makes her feel powerful and special—like she "tamed" him.

Scam move: Classic emotional bait. He creates the illusion of transformation to make her invest more, thinking she changed him. But really? He says that to **every woman** on the hook.

3. "You're Not Like the Others" Line

"I don't talk to nobody else the way I talk to you."
What he's doing:
This is a manipulation staple. He's making her feel exclusive in a system built on rotation.

Scam move: That line's been said a thousand times by a thousand men in a thousand yards. It's just emotional flattery to lock her deeper into the fantasy.

4. Erotic Fantasy Trap

"Laid up in a hotel… tank top, no panties… whisperin' in your ear…"
What he's doing:
He's painting a detailed sexual daydream—not just to turn her on, but to build emotional and physical addiction. Her body reacts. Her guard lowers. She feels bonded.

Scam move: This ain't just foreplay—it's financial grooming. He uses fantasy to keep her emotionally hooked and justify the next ask.

5. Future-Faking Distraction

"That's what I wanna give you. Everything."
What he's doing:
He sells her a dream future so she ignores the shit reality—he's broke, he's locked up, and she's payin' for everything.

Scam move: It's a down payment on a future that ain't comin'. The promise buys her loyalty now. He cashes it in through guilt and fantasy.

6. Emotional Validation Sandwich

"You the one thing that makes this time bearable… You got that raw energy…"
What he's doing:
He hits her with compliments that feel spiritual and sexy at the same time. Now her identity is tied to his happiness.

Scam move: This makes her feel like a lifeline—so when the ask comes, she feels obligated to help. After all, how can you let your "light" go dark?

7. Financial Softball (Guilt-Twist Request)

"I ain't tryna make this about money, but… I'm down to one soap…"
What he's doing:
Here it is. The whole letter's been foreplay for this moment. He's not "asking"—he's "just saying." He's framing it like an offhand, humble need.

Scam move: He's making the hustle sound casual so it doesn't trigger her defenses. It's guilt-wrapped in "If you can…," but the pressure is real.

8. The Flirty Closeout

"Can't wait for the day I slide my hands down your thighs..."
What he's doing:
He brings it back to the body. He ends with lust, connection, and more fantasy. Why? So she's too flustered to be mad about the money ask.

Scam move: It's psychological distraction. She finishes the letter feeling wanted, sexy, and loved—even though she just got finessed for $40 and a false future.

Kiesha's Final Reflections on Dre

Andre's not just runnin' game—he's running a **full emotional and sexual manipulation operation.** This is **not a love letter.** It's a scripted performance designed to get her **hooked emotionally and giving financially,** all while thinking she's in control.

Fictional Letter #6: "The Daddy's Demand"

From: DeShawn R. (#5518039)
Location: Unit E, South Wing – 24 Hour Lock
Date: November 11

To My Baby Girl,

Let me get one thing straight before I say anything else: **you mine.** I don't care what nobody out there says, I don't care what distractions come your way—I claimed you, and I stand on that. So if you ridin', then ride. If you driftin', pull your ass back before you crash this thing we built.

You think I don't notice the change in your energy? You shorter on the phone. You taking longer to write. You ain't saying my name the same. I peep all of that. And I ain't mad—I'm disappointed. We supposed to be locked in, girl. You told me you wanted a man who'd lead, who'd protect you, who'd make you feel safe. Well, here I am. But now you flinchin' every time I give you direction?

Nah. That's not how this work.

I don't ask for much. I don't need much. But what I expect is loyalty, consistency, and effort. I don't want some part-time pen pal—I want my woman. And if you mine, then act like it. I'm not gonna keep explainin' myself or askin' twice. You already know what I expect.

You also know I'm in a situation where I need to lean on you sometimes. That's part of the deal. I handle my business in here, I stay focused, I keep my name clean—and you hold it down out there. That's how we move. You want me out there with you one day? Then support me like you already got me.

I need you to slide $60 this week. That ain't me beggin', that's me planning. I got a few things I need to re-up on, and I ain't gon' sit around waitin' for handouts from people who don't matter. You the one who matter. You always said you got me, right? Then don't make me question it.

And while we at it, you better not be out there actin' single. I hear shit. Don't think it don't get back to me. If we locked in, then I shouldn't even have to say this—but I will: **you carry my name.** Don't play with that.

Now write me back soon. Not because I need to hear from you. Because it's your damn job to make sure I'm good. You mine, remember?

Daddy.

Kiesha's Final Reflections on DeShawn

You feel that? That letter ain't sweet. It's a damn **power grab wrapped in pet names.**
This ain't love—it's **a psychological collar**. He ain't trying to connect. He's trying to **own**.

Let me know when you want the breakdown, 'cause I'm about to snatch this "Daddy" act by the throat and show you how he runs his mouth like a boss while stealing your peace like a thief.

Ohhh hell yes. Let's drag **Daddy's manipulative ass** into the yard and break him down **like a damn shank search**. That letter? It ain't affection—it's **domination.**_It's "I love you" spelled with **control, ego, and thinly-veiled threats**. He's not askin' for love—he's demanding submission. Let me dissect this power move line by line.

1. Possessive Claim Opening

"You mine. I claimed you."
What he's doing:
He's not expressing love—he's laying **ownership**. Right from the jump, he removes her autonomy and rebrands her as his property.

Scam move: This ain't romance. This is psychological lockdown. It sets the tone: he owns the relationship, and she needs to act accordingly.

2. Emotional Guilt Twist

"You shorter on the phone. You taking longer to write. I ain't mad—I'm disappointed."
What he's doing:
This is a classic tactic. He flips subtle behavioral changes into betrayals. He don't yell—he guilt-trips, like a manipulative parent scolding a child.

Scam move: Makes her question herself. Makes her feel obligated to overcompensate. She'll write more, call faster, and send money just to get back in his "good graces."

3. Control Masquerading as Leadership

"You told me you wanted a man to lead, to protect... but now you flinchin' every time I give you direction?"
What he's doing:
He reframes his **control** as **leadership**. If she resists? She's the one with the problem.

Scam move: Gaslighting her into believing his control is actually her own request. He flips her desire for partnership into a reason to dominate her.

4. Shifting Responsibility Onto Her

"I stay focused in here, keep my name clean—you hold it down out there."

What he's doing:
He builds a **contract** where his survival is her job. She doesn't just "help" him—she owes it to him, as part of a fake loyalty pact.

Scam move: Makes her responsible for his financial and emotional needs, while he does nothing but sit in a cell and bark orders.

5. Financial Softball Disguised as Planning

"I need you to slide $60... that ain't me beggin', that's me planning."
What he's doing:
He distances himself from the idea of begging. Instead, he wraps the demand in purpose—as if it's part of some noble survival strategy.

Scam move: He's still **asking for money**, but disguises it as "us building together." It's financial coercion dressed as leadership.

6. Implying Threat With Jealousy Control

"You better not be out there actin' single... I hear shit."
What he's doing:
Now he shifts to fear tactics. He implies that if she's moving like she's single, **he'll know**—even from prison.

Scam move: Fear-based control. He implants paranoia in her mind. Now every interaction she has in the free world feels like she's "cheating."

7. Identity Hijack

"You carry my name."
What he's doing:
He strips her of personal identity. She's no longer her own woman—she's his property, his brand. She exists through him now.

Scam move: This deepens psychological control. It makes her feel like her choices don't just reflect on her—they "disrespect" him.

8. Commanding Tone Closer

"Write me back. Not because I need it—because it's your damn job."
What he's doing:
He ends not with love—but with **authority**. This ain't a relationship. It's a prison-built **hierarchy** where he sits on top and she's just expected to fall in line.

Scam move: He takes away her agency. Removes mutuality. It's no longer about connection—it's obligation, demand, and compliance.

Kiesha's Final Reflections on DeShawn

This letter wasn't written with love. It was written with a **mental chokehold**. Every line was about control. About **reminding her she don't belong to herself anymore**. He's not protecting her—he's **possessing** her.

This ain't Daddy. This is **Daddy-turned-Warden**, and if she ain't careful, she'll be doing a bid right alongside him—but hers will be emotional, financial, and invisible.

Fictional Letter #7 (Extended): "The Ghost's Return"

From: Malik S. (#4311707)
Location: B-Unit, Restricted Movement Tier
Date: November 18

Hey.

You probably wasn't expecting to hear from me. Hell, maybe you were. You always had that sixth sense when it came to me. That part of you that felt me even when I went quiet. You're probably sitting there wondering if you should even read this—or just tear it up and toss it. And if you do? I get it. I really do.

But if you're still readin'... thank you.
I ain't earned that.

I know I disappeared. Again.
 And I know what that does to you.
 I've felt your silence back. I know how it burns when the person you care about starts acting like a ghost   .
 But for me? I wasn't tryna hurt you. I was just tryna survive my own head.

See, in here, shit gets loud. And not in a physical way. The noise I deal with? It's in my chest. In my mind. And when it gets like that, I go into shutdown mode. I don't write. I don't call. I just... disappear. But not from you—just from myself.

You were the only thing that felt real when everything else felt like it was closing in.

That's why I kept your letters in my pillowcase. Reread your words like medicine. Even when I didn't answer, your voice stayed with me. Loud. Clear. Steady.

And I wanted to write. I did.
 But I didn't wanna drag you into my darkness.
 Not again.

The truth is—I get scared. Scared of you loving me too much. Scared of me not being enough. Scared of failing you, like I've failed everyone else who ever gave a fuck.
 So instead of holding you closer, I pull away.
 I know that don't make sense. I know it sounds stupid. But that's the broken part of me I don't show nobody... except you.

You deserve better than this. You deserve answers. You deserve consistency.

But I'm not built like them other dudes writing fairy tales from their bunk. I don't know how to fake forever. All I got is this moment, and right now?
 I'm reaching for you.

Not because I need something.
 Not because I want a favor.
 Just because I miss you.

I miss the way your voice slowed me down.
 I miss how you never asked me to be anyone but myself—even when that self was fucked up.
 I miss how you reminded me I could still be something... someone... more than this ID number and concrete.

And if you're still there—if you're still mine, even just a little—I want to fix what I broke. I want to try again, if you'll let me. But I'll understand if you won't.

Just don't think I ever stopped feeling you.
 You've been under my skin, in my thoughts, and in every breath I take after 10pm. That's when it hits the hardest.
 That's when your absence feels like punishment I actually earned.

I'll keep writing, if you let me.
 Even if it's just to say what I couldn't before.

Still haunted by you,
 Malik

Kiesha's Reflections On Malik

Now THAT'S The Ghost in full form. He says everything and nothing at the same time. He doesn't own his silence—he **romanticizes it**. He flips his disappearances into depth, his emotional absence into mystique, and his inability to commit into some tragic, poetic flaw.

But you want the breakdown, right? I'll rip this manipulative ghost-boy into shreds next and show every soft-spoken trick he used. Let's finish this. Let's go, girl. Time to drag this whisperin', moody-ass, emotionally evasive, manipulative motherfucker straight out of the shadows and into the damn light.

Malik ain't deep. He's just silent long enough for you to fill in the gaps with your own hope. He disappears, then reappears just soft enough to keep you holding on. You think you've got a soul connection, but what you really got is **a ghost that feeds off your love like it's a goddamn ration pack.** Let's tear him down piece by piece.

1. Strategic Vulnerability Opener

"You probably wasn't expecting to hear from me... And if you do? I get it. I really do."
 What he's doing:
 He opens with low-simmer guilt and false humility. He knows she's mad. He doesn't apologize—he pre-empts her anger by acknowledging it in a soft, non-confrontational way.

Scam move: He's resetting the clock. His absence gets brushed aside because he "gets it." But he doesn't own it—he uses it to make himself look thoughtful instead of accountable.

2. Emotional Withdrawal Justified

"I wasn't tryna hurt you... I was just tryna survive my own head."
What he's doing:
He's reframing emotional abandonment as deep, tortured introspection. Now he's not a flake—he's a wounded poet. He doesn't ghost because he's careless, he does it because he's "struggling."

Scam move: Romanticizing inconsistency. He turns red flags into tragic personality traits—and she starts nurturing him instead of leaving him.

3. "You Stayed Loud in My Head" Line

"Even when I didn't answer, your voice stayed with me..."
What he's doing:
He minimizes his silence by elevating her presence. She's his guiding light, his muse, his constant. Meanwhile, she was wondering if he died.

Scam move: He makes her feel important while completely skipping over the hurt she endured waiting for a damn reply.

4. Self-Sabotage Framed as Fear

"I get scared... of you loving me too much. Of not being enough."
What he's doing:
Here comes the sympathy bomb. He's not manipulative—he's just scared. Now she feels bad for setting boundaries or asking for consistency.

Scam move: Weaponized insecurity. He flips the script so she becomes the one reassuring him—even though he's the one who ghosted.

5. Fake Accountability With No Change

"You deserve better than this... But I'm not built like them other dudes..."
What he's doing:
He drops just enough self-awareness to seem real—but he never offers a solution. He's admitting the problem without changing a damn thing.

Scam move: It's false growth. He sounds emotionally mature, but it's just lip service to keep her hoping he might "evolve."

6. Passive "I Miss You" Manipulation

"Not because I need something... just because I miss you."
What he's doing:
He deliberately says he's not asking for anything—just to make the emotional pull feel purer. But don't get it twisted—this is a setup.

Scam move: This is emotional re-entry. He's rebuilding the connection so he can ask for something next week, and she'll say yes without question.

7. Nostalgia Control

"I miss the way your voice slowed me down... You never asked me to be anyone but myself..."
What he's doing:
He's dragging her back into the moments where she felt needed and special. Now she's emotionally locked back in before she can process the bullshit he just put her through.

Scam move: Weaponizing memories. He stirs up the highlight reel and erases the low points.

8. Reappearing Without Rebuilding

"If you're still mine, even just a little, I want to fix what I broke."
What he's doing:
He offers redemption without action. He wants forgiveness without work. He wants back in the door without building trust.

Scam move: That's not growth—it's **emotional loitering.** He ain't rebuilding. He's just lingering.

9. Romanticizing Absence

"You've been under my skin... your absence feels like punishment I earned."
What he's doing:

He plays both sides: you're a blessing, but your silence is punishment. This keeps her emotionally unsure—torn between staying mad and feeling needed.

Scam move: This line hits hard because it manipulates her empathy. Suddenly he's the victim of her boundaries.

Kiesha's Final Reflections on Malik

He don't come loud. He comes low. Soft. Quiet. Smooth. He haunts, not hounds._But his silence is a weapon, and his reappearance is **pure manipulation dressed as emotional depth.** He don't need to ask for money. He just needs to get back in her heart—because once he's there, she'll hand over the keys to everything without him even asking.

Keisha's Closing Notes

Alright, ladies—let's keep it all the way real. You just read seven letters, seven styles, seven different hustles wrapped in lace, scripture, thug-love, and fake vulnerability. And guess what? Every single one of them ended in the same damn place: **your wallet, your loyalty, your energy.**

Don't get it twisted—these dudes ain't writing love. They're writing scripts. You weren't chosen because you're special—you were chosen because you're reachable. That's the cold truth nobody wants to admit.

Read those letters again if you have to. See the patterns. Hear the tone. Notice how every "baby I love you" is just a runway for "slide me forty on JPay." Notice how every "God sent you to me" is just a warm-up for guilt when you don't answer quick enough. Notice how every promise of a future is really just a leash to keep you stuck in their present.

This is psychological warfare, not romance. And the battlefield ain't prison—it's your heart.

So here's my bottom line: if any letter in this module felt **too familiar**, you're not in love—you're in a con. And the only way to win a con is to walk away before it bleeds you dry.

Don't argue with me. Don't defend him. Don't say "he's not like that." Because if you felt that gut punch while reading, then yeah—he's exactly like that. Close the chapter. Close the JPay app. Close the door on his hustle. And for once in your life, close it in a way he can't reopen.

—**Keisha**

CON GAMES MODULE FIVE

Self-Assessment: Are You Being Played?

30 Questions to Spot the Manipulation

Instructions:

Answer **Yes** or **No** to each question. Count how many **Yes** responses you get at the end.

Then go check the *Keisha Meter of Manipulation* below.

1–10: The Emotional Bait

1. Does he guilt-trip you for missing calls or visits?
2. Has he ever cried on the phone, then asked for money?
3. Do you feel *bad* when you say no to him?
4. Has he ever called you "selfish" for setting boundaries?
5. Does he only open up emotionally right before commissary?
6. Do his moods shift depending on how much you're giving?
7. Has he ever said, "You're all I have," to keep you hooked?
8. Do you feel more like a therapist than a partner?
9. Does he bring up his trauma as a reason for his behavior?
10. Do you keep secrets about the relationship from your friends?

11–20: The Financial Drain

11. Are you sending money on a regular basis?
12. Have you skipped a bill to send him something?
13. Has he ever said, "I didn't ask you to," while still expecting help?
14. Does he get mad or go quiet when you don't send something?
15. Have you bought things for his family or friends?
16. Has he asked you to contact someone *on his behalf* for money?
17. Do you feel obligated to send gifts, packages, or photos?
18. Has he ever said you're not "holding it down" enough?

19. Do you know his DOC number better than your own account balance?
20. Have you ever lied to yourself about how much you're spending?

21–30: The Identity Erosion

21. Do you feel like you've lost who you were before him?
22. Have your goals, routines, or self-care taken a backseat to his needs?
23. Are you afraid to bring up your concerns to him?
24. Do you walk on eggshells during calls or visits?
25. Do you find yourself defending him to everyone, even when you're unsure?
26. Has he told you "nobody else will love you like I do"?
27. Do you fantasize about the future more than enjoy the present?
28. Have you made big life decisions based on *his* timeline or release date?
29. Do you feel exhausted—mentally, emotionally, financially?
30. Deep down, do you know something ain't right, but you're scared to admit it?

Keisha's Meter of Manipulation:

- **0–5 Yes**

  You're good—for now. Stay sharp. Keep them boundaries tight and don't let the charm override your common sense.

- **6–15 Yes**

  You're in the *danger zone*. He's got some kind of hold on you—emotional, financial, or mental. Start checking yourself *before* it goes deeper.

- **16–25 Yes**

  Girl, you're in a full-blown *prison romance trap*. This ain't love—it's a hustle in disguise. You're doing the time, and he's calling the shots.

- **26–30 Yes**

  Pull the fire alarm. You're being emotionally pimped out and he's runnin' your life from behind bars. This is your *intervention*. You need to ghost his ass, get your power back, and rebuild—*now*.

Keisha's Reflections

This assessment ain't here to shame you—it's here to set you *free*. If the answers hurt, good. That means the truth's gettin' through. Let me know if you want this turned into a printable worksheet or part of the back of the book. I'll make it clean but still savage.

CON GAMES MODULE SIX
Prison Hustle Definitions

1. JPay Queen

The unofficial ATM. Sends money religiously through JPay and gets breadcrumbs of attention in return.

2. Commissary Trap

The guilt-trip hustle—"I ain't got no soap, baby"—so you fund his snacks and hygiene while he romances someone else with your ramen.

3. Store Day Romance

He loves you heavy the week before commissary. Once he's stocked up, he goes ghost like Houdini.

4. Ride-or-Die Chick

You're labeled this so he can make you feel special while keeping you locked in a loyalty contract he don't follow.

5. Holding It Down

The phrase he uses to keep you stuck. Translation: "Don't ask questions. Just pay and wait."

6. The Fantasy Future

His prison love script. Wedding, house, kids—none of which he's planning to deliver.

7. Call Time Guilt Trip

You miss a call and suddenly you're disloyal. It's emotional manipulation 101.

8. Mailbox Game

He sends poetic letters with just enough sweetness to keep you hooked. Most of them are recycled lines from his "pen pal playbook."

9. Picture Package Bait

He begs for sexy pics to "feel connected." Then trades or sells them to other inmates. Yup. Welcome to the prison marketplace.

10. Pen Pal Pyramid Scheme

One man. Multiple women. All thinking they're "the one." He rotates attention based on who's paying best.

11. The Loyalty Test

He picks fights to see how far you'll go to prove you "ride." It's all about control.

12. The Release Lie

He claims he's getting out early. He ain't. But you'll keep sending money thinking you're investing in a future.

13. The Cellblock Switch-Up

Sudden mood swings and "I need space" texts. Usually tied to another chick or a busted hustle.

14. State Soap Struggle

The sob story he gives you about having to use state-issued soap. Guilt bait for a $50 "hygiene emergency."

15. Down Ass Bitch

His term for the most loyal and blind supporter. Usually the one getting played the hardest.

16. Stand By Chick

The backup girl. He calls when his main chick gets tired of the BS. You're basically the benchwarmer.

17. Release Countdown Hype

The fake excitement build-up before his "release"—used to squeeze more money and promises outta you.

18. Mailroom Magic

What he calls the ability to charm women with letters. Real slick talk. Real fake intentions.

19. Con Call Chemistry

The illusion of connection built over 15-minute prison calls. Feels deep, but it's carefully calculated.

20. Commissary King

The inmate who lives good because five women are footing the bill. Always clean, always eatin' good.

21. Soft Hustle

When he plays the emotional victim instead of aggressive demands—"I hate asking you, but…"

22. The Slammer Sweetheart

What you think you are to him. But really, you're just the latest on his cellblock roster.

23. Cellblock Therapy

When he trauma-dumps to create false intimacy. "Nobody ever listened like you…" Heard that before?

24. Inmate Intimacy

The emotional addiction you develop to texts, calls, and attention that feels real—but is transactional.

25. Release Date Dangle

He keeps mentioning how close he is to getting out—to keep your hopes (and your money) up.

26. Commissary Co-Signer

His financial ride-or-die. If he ain't got it, you better. You basically become the prison Costco.

27. State Blues Fantasy

When you romanticize his situation—thinking being locked up makes him deep, loyal, or different. Sis, it don't.

28. The Call Collector

He lines up back-to-back calls with different chicks. You think you're special. You're just on the Tuesday rotation.

29. The Snail Mail Seducer

Master of letters. Real poetic. Real sweet. Real fake. Half the time, his celly's helping him write 'em.

30. The Commissary Cold Shoulder

When you don't send money, he suddenly needs "time to think" or "process his mental health."

31. Locked-In Lies

The bullshit timeline of promises: "When I get out, we'll…"—it's all hopes, no plans.

32. The Shift

When he stops being loving and starts being controlling. Usually happens once he knows you're hooked.

33. The D.O.C. Dangler

Drops Department of Corrections policy talk like he's a damn lawyer. Used to confuse and distract you from his shady behavior.

34. Honeybun Honeymoon

That first 2 months of letters, poems, and good behavior before the manipulation begins. Enjoy it—it's bait.

35. Watchdog Wifey

He turns you into his spy. Wants to know where you are, who you talk to, what you wear—*from prison*.

36. Fed Fantasy

When he claims he's a political prisoner or misunderstood rebel. Naw, sis. He sold dope. Don't let the poetry fool you.

37. The Cry Call

Tears on the phone. Real or fake, used to manipulate. "You don't love me like you used to…" Cue the Cash App.

38. Dirty Drawers Defense

He claims someone stole his underwear or food to guilt you into "helping him survive." Dramatic as hell.

39. The Bunkie Bounce

He gets caught cheating with another woman—then blames it on his bunkie sending the wrong letter or email. Classic.

40. Broke Bae Breakdown

When you finally say no, and he turns cold, bitter, and petty. Love disappears the moment the money does.

CON GAMES MODULE SEVEN

Prison Slang Dictionary

Why You Need to Know This!!!

Ladies, let me break it down plain: words behind those walls don't mean what they mean out here. You can stroll in with your college degree, your polished vocabulary, and your perfect grammar—but in prison, that makes you sound like a tourist. And tourists get robbed.

Prison slang is more than talk—it's currency, it's camouflage, and it's a weapon. One wrong word, and you can end up marked as weak, fake, or clueless. And trust me, those labels stick. You don't want to be the woman who giggles at a word you don't understand or asks the wrong question in front of the wrong people. That's not cute—that's dangerous.

This dictionary is your crash course. I'm not saying you gotta memorize it and walk around talking like you just stepped off the yard. But you damn sure need to recognize it. Why? Because every letter you get, every phone call you take, every "baby I love you" whispered through the receiver might be laced with slang that's saying more than you realize. If you don't speak the code, you won't catch the play. And if you don't catch the play, you're the one getting played.

Think of it like this: the language is part of the hustle. If you don't know it, you can't see the hustle coming. Period.

So read this section like your heart and your wallet depend on it—because they do. Don't get caught slipping, don't get caught guessing, and for God's sake, don't ever be the one who asks out loud what "CHOMO" means. That's not a lesson you want to learn in real time.

This ain't about sounding hard. It's about staying smart. Let's get you fluent before you get fluent in regret.

—Keisha

Your New Vocabulary

A-B-C Check (*ay-bee-see chek*): A test of loyalty or intelligence.

Ace Boon (*ays-boon*): Best friend or close ally. "That's his ace boon; they're inseparable."

Agitator (*aj-i-tay-tor*): Someone who stirs up trouble. "He's an agitator, always starting fights in the pod."

All Day (*awl day*): Life sentence. "He's doing all day for that murder charge."

Aunt Sally (*awnt sal-ee*): A nickname for the government or prison administration.

Baby Mama Drama (*bay-bee mah-mah drah-mah*): Issues caused by an inmate's partner or ex

Back Door (bak dor): Escape route or hidden exit. "He's planning to use the back door during the transfer."

Bad Paper (bad pay-per): False or unreliable legal documents. "He got bad paper, and now nobody trusts him."

Bagged (bag-d): Caught doing something wrong. "He got bagged hiding contraband."

Bam Bam (bam-bam): Homemade weapon used in a fight. "He swung a bam bam during the brawl."

Bang Up (bang up): Solitary confinement. "They sent him to bang up after the fight."

Beastin' (beest-in): Acting wild or out of control. "He's been beastin' ever since he got that extra time."

Beef (beef): Conflict or charge. "He's got a beef with another inmate over commissary."

Belly Chain (bel-ee chayn): Restraints used during transport. "They cuffed him with a belly chain for the transfer."

Bid (bid): Prison sentence. "He's doing a five-year bid for armed robbery."

Blackout (blak-out): Complete loss of privileges. "They gave the whole unit a blackout after the riot."

Blades (blayds): Sharp weapons. "They found two blades hidden in his cell."

Bluebird (bloo-burd): A letter from home. "He was excited to get a bluebird this morning."

Bone Crusher (bohn krush-er): A large, lethal homemade weapon.

Boneyard (boh-nee-yard): Conjugal visit area. "He's excited for time in the boneyard this weekend."

Boomerang (boo-mer-ang): Inmate who keeps coming back to prison.

Boss Up (baws up): To take control or act tough. "He had to boss up to earn respect."

Brace Up (brays up): Prepare for a fight or trouble. "He braced up when they approached him."

Break it Down (brayk it down): Explain or simplify. "Break it down for the new fish so he understands."

Buck Fifty (buk fif-tee): A knife wound across the face. "He gave his enemy a buck fifty in the yard."

Bug (buhg): Mentally unstable person. "That guy's a bug—don't mess with him."

Bullet (bull-it): A one-year sentence. "He's only serving a bullet; he'll be out soon."

Bunkie (bunk-ee): Cellmate. "My bunkie snores all night."

Burned (burn-d): Betrayed or exposed. "He got burned by his own crew."

Burnt (burnt): No longer useful or trustworthy. "He's burnt in this car after talking to the C.O."

Burpee Check (bur-pee chek): A physical endurance test.

C.O. (see-oh): Correctional officer. "The C.O. searched the cells this morning."

Canteen Cowboy (kan-teen kow-boy): Inmate who flaunts commissary items to gain favor.

Cap (kap): A lie or exaggeration. "That story about him running the yard is pure cap."

Car (kar): Gang or group. "He runs with the white car in the yard."

Catch a Case (kach uh kays): To get charged with a new crime. "He caught a case for assault while inside."

Catch a Chain (kach-uh-chayn): Be transferred to another prison. "He's catching a chain tomorrow morning."

Cellie (sell-ee): Cellmate. "My cellie keeps stealing my soap."

Chain Gang (chayn gang): Group of prisoners working together, often while shackled.

Check Off (chek awf): Voluntary removal from the yard or group to avoid harm.

Checked (chekt): Challenged or confronted. "He got checked for not paying his debts."

Chi-Chi (chee-chee): A special dish made from commissary items.

Chomo (choh-moh): Child molester. "Chomos get handled quick in here."

Chow (chow): Meal or cafeteria. "Chow time is at 5 PM sharp."

Commissary (kom-uh-sair-ee): Prison store. "I need to stock up at commissary today."

Contraband (kon-truh-band): Forbidden items. "He was caught with contraband during inspection."

Count (kownt): Inmate headcount. "Everyone froze during the count."

Crash Dummy (krash dum-ee): Inmate manipulated into dangerous situations.

Cutthroat (kut-throht): Ruthless or untrustworthy inmate. "Watch out for him; he's a cutthroat."

Dead Man Walking (ded man wah-king): Inmate on death row.

Dead Presidents (ded prez-i-dents): Money. "He's always hustling for some dead presidents."

Dead Time (ded tym): Time served without parole or reduction. "He's doing dead time until his release date."

Diesel Therapy (dee-zuhl ther-uh-pee): Punishment by repeated transfers.

Dime (dym): A 10-year sentence. "He's doing a dime for drug trafficking."

Dog Food (dawg food): Heroin. "They caught him trying to smuggle dog food into the yard."

Dope Fiend Move (dohp feend moov): Deceptive or sneaky behavior.

Double Up (duh-buhl up): Sharing a cell designed for one person.

Down (down): To serve time. "He's been down for 10 years already."

Down Bad (down bad): In a tough or desperate situation. "He's down bad after losing his commissary."

Down to Ride (down too ryd): Loyal to the group. "He's always down to ride for his car."

Draino (dray-noh): A strong drink made in prison. "They cooked up some Draino for the celebration."

Drift (drift): To slowly move away from a gang or group. "He's starting to drift from his car."

Dry Snitching (dry snitch-ing): Revealing information without directly naming names.

Duffle Bag Boy (duhf-uhl bag boy): Someone carrying drugs. "He's the duffle bag boy for the crew."

Eight Ball (ayt bawl): A small amount of drugs, typically cocaine.

Face Card (fays kard): Someone's reputation or credibility. "His face card is solid in this prison."

Fence Jumper (fens jump-er): Inmate who switches gangs or alliances.

Fish (fish): New inmate. "The fish doesn't know anything yet."

Fish Kit (fish kit): Starter pack given to new inmates. "They handed him a fish kit with soap and a toothbrush."

Fish Tank (fish tank): A cellblock for new arrivals. "They put him in the fish tank until he learns the rules."

Flat Time (flat tym): A sentence without parole. "He's serving flat time with no chance of early release."

Flex (fleks): To show off or boast. "He's flexing with all that commissary."

Flopped (flopt): Failed parole or appeal. "He flopped his hearing and got five more years."

Footwork (foot-werk): Effort put into gang activities. "He's putting in footwork for his crew."

Freelance (free-lans): An inmate without gang ties. "He's freelancing to avoid drama."

Freight Train (frayt trayn): Overwhelming attack. "He got hit with a freight train during the riot."

Full House (ful hows): Cell overcrowding. "We've got a full house in this block now."

Gaffle (gaf-uhl): To grab or take by force. "The C.O.s gaffled him during the raid."

Gate Money (gayt muh-nee): Money given upon release. "He used his gate money to grab a bus ticket."

Ghost Rider (gohst ryd-er): Someone who acts tough but avoids real action.

Ghosted (gohst-ed): Left without notice or disappeared. "He ghosted from the yard after the fight."

Gorilla (guh-ril-uh): A strong, aggressive inmate. "That gorilla runs the shower room."

Green Light (green lite): Attack order. "The shot-caller gave a green light on him."

Grievance (gree-vuhns): Formal complaint filed by an inmate. "He filed a grievance about the food quality."

Gump (guhmp): Homosexual inmate. "That gump stays out of trouble in here."

Hacks (haks): Slang for correctional officers. "The hacks are patrolling the tier tonight."

Heat (heet): Increased attention from authorities. "They're laying low because there's too much heat."

Hold Your Mud (hold yur mud): Maintain composure under pressure. "He held his mud during the interrogation."

Hole (hole): Solitary confinement. "He's been in the hole for fighting."

Homeboy (hohm-boy): Someone from the same area or neighborhood.

Hooch (hooch): Homemade alcohol. "They found hooch brewing in the laundry room."

Hot Seat (hot seet): Being in trouble or under scrutiny. "He's in the hot seat after the C.O. found his stash."

House Mouse (hows mows): An inmate who cleans for the guards.

Ice Pick (ys pik): A sharp weapon made for stabbing. "He keeps an ice pick hidden in his mattress."

In the Mix (in thuh miks): Being involved in prison politics or action. "He's always in the mix, never sitting still."

Inside Man (in-syd man): Someone working within a system to provide information.

Iron Pile (i-urn pyle): Weightlifting equipment. "He spends all his rec time at the iron pile."

Jack (jak): To steal. "He jacked someone's commissary last night."

Jackpot (jak-pot): Major trouble or big find. "He hit the jackpot when he found that stash."

Jackrabbit (jak-rab-it): Inmate who tries to escape. "He's a known jackrabbit—always looking for a way out."

Jailhouse Lawyer (jayl-hows loy-er): An inmate who helps others with legal issues.

Jody (joe-dee): Someone on the outside dating your partner. "Jody's with his wife while he's locked up."

Jolt (johl-t): A long prison sentence. "He's serving a jolt for armed robbery."

Juice (joos): Power, respect, or influence. "That guy has juice in this facility."

Jumped (jump-d): Attacked by a group. "He got jumped in the yard yesterday."

K.O.S. (kay-oh-es): Kill on sight. "He's got a K.O.S. order from his car."

Kangaroo Court (kan-guh-roo kort): Informal prison justice.

Kite (kite): Secret note. "Pass this kite to someone in the next pod."

Kite Runner (kyt ruhn-er): Someone who delivers secret notes.

Lame Duck (laym duhk): An inmate without allies or power. "He's a lame duck; nobody has his back."

Lawnmower (lawn-mo-er): Someone who runs errands for others.

Lick (lik): A successful hustle or theft. "He hit a lick selling stolen commissary."

Lifer (lye-fur): Life sentence inmate. "The lifers control the yard rules."

Lockdown (lok-down): Prison-wide restriction of movement. "We've been on lockdown all week."

Lollipop (lol-ee-pop): Someone easily manipulated. "They treat him like a lollipop, taking advantage of him."

Mad Dogging (mad dog-ing): Intense staring or glaring to intimidate.

Meat Wagon (meet wag-in): Prison transport vehicle or ambulance.

Monkey Suit (mun-kee soot): Prison uniform. "He hates wearing that monkey suit all day."

Moonshine (moon-shyn): Illegally brewed alcohol. "They're brewing moonshine in the mop closet again."

Mule (mule): Person who smuggles contraband. "They caught the mule during visitation."

Nickel (nik-ul): A five-year sentence. "He's doing a nickel for armed robbery."

No Hands (noh handz): Refusing to fight or defend oneself. "They called him no hands after he backed down."

Nod Out (nod owt): To fall asleep, often from drug use. "He nodded out after using dog food."

Nortenos (nor-tay-nos): Northern California gang network affiliated with the Nuestra Familia

Off the Count (awf-thuh-kownt): Missing during inmate headcount. "He went off the count caused lockdown."

Off the Hook (awf the hook): Out of control or chaotic. "The tier was off the hook after lockdown."

On Deck (awn dek): Ready or available. "He's on deck to handle any problems."

P.C. (pee-see): Protective custody. "They sent him to P.C. after the threats got serious."

Paper Chaser (pay-pur chay-sir): Someone focused on making money.

Paperwork (pay-pur-work): Legal documents proving charges. "Show your paperwork, or they won't trust you."

Peckerwood (pek-er-wood): White inmate or gang member. "That peckerwood runs with the Aryans."

Pill Line (pill lyn): Line for receiving medication. "He's always in the pill line for his anxiety meds."

Playing Possum (play-ing poss-um): Pretending to be unaware or weak.

Pod (pod): Section of a prison. "We're moving to the next pod after lunch."

Program (proh-gram): Routine or self-improvement. "He's programming hard to stay out of trouble."

Pull Rank (pul rank): To use status to control others. "The shot-caller pulled rank to settle the dispute."

Punk (puhnk): Weak or submissive inmate. "They turned him into a punk after he owed money."

Rabbit (rab-it): An inmate prone to escape attempts. "They keep an eye on him; he's a rabbit."

Rec (rek): Recreational time. "We get rec in the yard after lunch."

Ride the Beef (ryd thuh beef): Serve time for a specific charge. "

Ride the Fence (ryd the fens): Avoiding taking sides in conflicts.

Roll (rohl): To inform or testify. "He rolled on his entire crew to get a deal."

Roll Up (rohl up): Pack belongings for transfer. "He's rolling up tomorrow to a new facility."

Run It (run it): Demand or take something. "He told the fish to run it or get handled."

Running Numbers (ruh-ning num-burs): Gamblin

Sack (sak): Bag of commissary items. "He's trading his sack for hygiene products."

Shakedown (shake-down): Cell search. "They're doing a shakedown after count."

Shank (shank): Homemade weapon. "He made a shank out of a toothbrush."

Shiv (shiv): A homemade stabbing weapon. "He got caught with a shiv during the shakedown."

Short Timer (short tym-er): Inmate close to release. "He's a short timer with 30 days left."

Shot-Caller (shot-kaw-ler): Gang leader. "The shot-caller gave the green light."

Slam Dunk (slam dunk): A sure or obvious outcome. "The green light on him was a slam dunk."

Slammer (slam-er): Prison. "He's been in the slammer for five years now."

Smoke (smohk): Trouble or conflict. "He doesn't want any smoke with the shot-caller."

Snitch (snitch): Informant. "Snitches don't last long in here."

South Siders (south-sy-ders): Southern California gang network affiliated with the Mexican Mafia (La Eme).

Spread (spred): Meal made from commissary. "We're making a spread for dinner tonight."

Square (skwair): Someone who avoids illegal activity or prison politics.

Stay Down (stay down): Remain loyal or consistent. "You've got to stay down for your people."

Steppin' (step-in): Acting aggressively or with purpose. "He's steppin' to prove he belongs in the crew."

Store Box (stor boks): Excess commissary items. "He's got a full store box in his cell."

Sureños (sue-ray-nyos): Southern California gang alliance controlled by Mexican Mafia (La Eme).

Tank (tank): Holding cell. "They're keeping him in the tank until the transfer."

Tank Boss (tank bawss): Leader of a cellblock. "The tank boss runs the pod with an iron fist."

Tapped Out (tapt owt): Out of money or resources.

Tattoo Gun (tat-too gun): Improvised tattooing device. "He's got a tattoo gun made from a pen and motor."

Thick (thik): Heavy gang or political involvement. "He's thick with the Aryan car in this yard."

Ticket (tick-it): Disciplinary write-up. "He got a ticket for mouthing off to a C.O."

Top Dog (top dawg): The inmate in charge of a group or car. "The top dog made the call to handle the situation."

Torpedo (tor-pee-doh): An enforcer or someone sent to attack. "The torpedo handled the green light in the yard."

Turf (terf): A gang's area of control. "They're fighting over turf in the yard."

Turn Out (turn owt): To force someone into submission, often sexually. "He turned out the fish on his first day."

Under the Gun (uhn-der the gun): Under pressure or scrutiny. "He's under the gun after losing that package."

Walk Alone (wahk uh-lone): Inmate without affiliations. "He walks alone to stay out of politics."

Wall Kites (wawl kyts): Messages passed along walls or hidden areas.

Washed Up (wah-sht up): Lost respect or status. "He's washed up after years in protective custody."

Weak Sauce (week saws): Someone who lacks strength or courage. "That move was weak sauce—he'll regret it."

Wheel Man (weel man): Leader or boss. "The wheel man decides who gets the green light."

Whistle (whis-l): Warning or alarm. "He gave a whistle when the C.O. approached."

Work (werk): Drugs or illegal tasks. "He's pushing work for his car."

Wrecked (rekt): Beaten or destroyed. "He got wrecked in the fight yesterday."

Yard (yard): Outdoor area. "The yard is open after count."

Yard Dawg (yard dawg): Someone who dominates the yard. "That yard dawg controls all the action."

Yard Rat (yard rat): Inmate who spends all their time in the yard.

Zip (zip): An ounce of drugs. "He's moving zips to make commissary money."

Zipperhead (zip-er-hed): Inmate who self-harms. "He's known as a zipperhead for his scars."

Here's a list of the most popular and vulgar swear words commonly heard in prison, along with a bit of context for each. Because let's be real—prison conversations are often spiced with language you wouldn't use in Sunday school.

The Usual Suspects:

"Fuck"

The Swiss Army knife of prison profanity. It can be an insult, a threat, or even a term of endearment depending on the tone.

Example: *"Fuck off!"* or *"You fucked that up, didn't you?"*

"Shit"

A staple for expressing frustration, disbelief, or as a noun for contraband.

Example: *"This shit's getting out of hand."*

"Ass"

Used to insult someone, reference trouble (*"busted my ass"*), or describe a coward (*"punk-ass bitch"*).

Example: *"Move your ass before I move it for you."*

"Bitch"

Highly derogatory when aimed at another inmate—fighting words in many contexts. Also used to describe tasks or situations.

Example: *"That guard's a straight-up bitch."* or *"This workout is a bitch."*

"Motherfucker"

The ultimate insult or emphasis word. Used creatively and often.

Example: *"That motherfucker owes me commissary."*

Prison-Specific Favorites:

"Punk"

A deeply offensive term implying weakness or submission, often in a sexual context.

Example: *"Don't let anyone call you a punk unless you're ready to throw hands."*

"CHOMO"

Short for child molester. Universally despised and one of the most vulgar terms in prison. Just hearing it can spark violence.

Example: *"Don't even talk to that CHOMO."*

"Snitch"

While not a swear word in the traditional sense, it's one of the most damning labels you can earn.

Example: *"That snitch isn't gonna last long."*

Creative Combos and Add-ons:

"Cocksucker"

Rarely meant literally; it's an all-purpose insult for anyone who pisses you off.

Example: *"That cocksucker stole my commissary."*

"Douchebag"

Common in modern slang, it's made its way into prison lingo as a less intense insult.

Example: *"Quit being a douchebag and do your own laundry."*

"Dickhead"

Straightforward and to the point, this one is often used for annoying inmates or guards.

Example: *"That dickhead guard is on shift tonight."*

"Piss-ant"

A lesser-known insult for someone seen as petty or insignificant.

Example: *"Don't worry about that piss-ant; he's not worth your time."*

Extreme Slurs and Warnings

"Fag/Faggot"

A deeply offensive and outdated slur still used by ignorant inmates. Its use can spark arguments or fights.

"Fish"

Not vulgar but often used derogatorily toward new inmates.

Example: *"You're just a fish; you don't know shit yet."*

School's Out!!!

Alright, ladies—you just walked through a whole damn crash course in prison talk. Some of it's funny, some of it's filthy, and all of it matters. Because in that world, words ain't just conversation—they're signals, warnings, and tests.

Swearing isn't just about words—it's about context. In prison, the wrong word at the wrong time can escalate into something much bigger. Understanding the meaning and weight behind these terms can help you avoid unnecessary conflicts and stay in control of your interactions.

Pro Tip: Don't overuse profanity. Swearing every other word makes you sound like a fool, and in prison, nobody respects a fool. Save it for when it really matters, and you'll get your point across loud and clear.

Now let's be real: you don't need to run around dropping every term in this book. If you try too hard, you'll sound fake as hell, and fake gets spotted quick. What you do need is to recognize it when it's thrown your way. That's the difference between catching the hustle early or getting dragged for months before you realize you've been played.

This slang shows up in letters, on phone calls, in casual talk—always wrapped in some sweet story or hard-ass attitude. If you don't know the code, you won't see the hook until it's already in your skin. And once it's in? Good luck pulling it out without bleeding.

So here's my bottom line: study this, keep it close, and don't ever let somebody make you feel stupid for asking questions in private. Learn the language before the language learns you. Because in prison politics, sounding clueless ain't harmless—it's dangerous.

Stay sharp, stay smart, and don't let words become the rope they use to pull you under.

CON GAMES MODULE EIGHT

Index of Major Prison Gangs

The Players Who Run the Prison Yards

Major prison gangs in the U.S. are highly organized groups that operate both within the prison system and outside in the community. They are often regionally based and identifiable by tattoos, codes, hand signs, and affiliations. Here's a breakdown of some of the most prominent ones, their areas of influence, and how they can be recognized:

Spotting Prison Gang Members

- **Tattoos:** Key symbols, numbers, and imagery specific to the gang.
- **Colors:** Certain colors may indicate gang affiliation (e.g., red for Bloods, blue for Crips).
- **Language:** Use of gang codes, slang, or secretive communication methods.
- **Behavior:** Gang members often stick together in groups and display deference to high-ranking members.
- **Graffiti:** Tags in prison cells, on personal items, or walls to claim territory or send messages.

1. Aryan Brotherhood (AB)

- **Origin:** San Quentin State Prison, California (1960s)
- **Operations:** Nationwide, primarily in federal and state prisons.
- **Ideology:** White supremacy and organized crime.
- **Activities:** Drug trafficking, extortion, murder-for-hire, and protection rackets.
- **Identifying Features:**
  - Tattoos with shamrocks, swastikas, double lightning bolts, or the letters "AB."

- Numbers "666" or "88" (88 = HH = Heil Hitler).
- Often display strong loyalty to white supremacist ideologies.

2. Black Guerrilla Family (BGF)

- **Origin:** San Quentin State Prison, California (1966)
- **Operations:** Predominantly in California and Maryland.
- **Ideology:** Revolutionary, Marxist, anti-government.
- **Activities:** Drug trafficking, violence against rival gangs and law enforcement.
- **Identifying Features:**
  - Symbols like a dragon surrounding a prison tower.
  - The initials "BGF" or references to George Jackson, a founding member.
  - Focus on loyalty and secrecy.

3. Mexican Mafia (La Eme)

- **Origin:** Deuel Vocational Institution, California (1950s)
- **Operations:** Southern California and the Southwest; active in federal and state prisons.
- **Ideology:** Mexican-American pride, organized crime.
- **Activities:** Drug distribution, murder, extortion, human trafficking.
- **Identifying Features:**
  - Tattoos of a black handprint (La Mano Negra) or the letter "M."
  - Use of Spanish language and numbers associated with the letter M (e.g., 13 = M is the 13th letter).

4. Nuestra Familia (NF)

- **Origin:** Soledad Prison, California (1960s)
- **Operations:** Northern California; rivals to the Mexican Mafia.
- **Ideology:** Protect northern Mexican-Americans (Norteños) and oppose La Eme.
- **Activities:** Drug trafficking, extortion, violent retaliation against rivals.
- **Identifying Features:**
  - Symbols of a sombrero with a machete or the number "14" (N is the 14th letter).

- The color red to signify Norteño affiliation.
- Tattoos or graffiti with the letter "N" or "ENE."

5. Texas Syndicate (TS)

- **Origin:** Folsom Prison, California (1970s)
- **Operations:** Predominantly in Texas but also in federal prisons.
- **Ideology:** Protection of Texan inmates; no specific racial affiliation.
- **Activities:** Drug trafficking, extortion, violence.
- **Identifying Features:**
  - Tattoos with "TS," "Texas," or images of Texas-themed iconography (e.g., Longhorns).
  - Gang-affiliated members are often recruited through regional ties.

6. Bloods and Crips

- **Origin:** Los Angeles street gangs (1970s) that have moved into prison systems.
- **Operations:** Nationwide, particularly in urban areas.
- **Ideology:** Based on loyalty to their respective sets (Crips are blue, Bloods are red).
- **Activities:** Drug trafficking, robbery, extortion, and violent rivalries.
- **Identifying Features:**
  - Bloods wear red; Crips wear blue.
  - Tattoos and graffiti using gang-specific codes or numbers (e.g., "5" for Bloods, "6" for Crips).
  - Specific hand signs unique to each set.

7. MS-13 (Mara Salvatrucha)

- **Origin:** Los Angeles (1980s), primarily among Salvadoran immigrants.
- **Operations:** Nationwide but strongest in California, New York, and Central America.
- **Ideology:** Extreme violence to maintain control and loyalty.
- **Activities:** Murder, drug trafficking, extortion, human trafficking.

- **Identifying Features:**
    - Elaborate tattoos, often covering the face and body, including "MS," "13," or "Salvatrucha."
    - Use of machetes in violent acts.
    - Symbols of the devil, horns, or Gothic lettering.

8. Sureños (Sur 13)

- **Origin:** Southern California (aligned with the Mexican Mafia).
- **Operations:** Southern California, federal prisons, and border states.
- **Ideology:** Loyalty to the Mexican Mafia; rivals of Norteños.
- **Activities:** Drug trafficking, extortion, violent enforcement.
- **Identifying Features:**
    - Tattoos with "SUR," "13," or "XIII."
    - Blue clothing and symbols like the Aztec sun or a Mexican eagle.

9. Barrio Azteca

- **Origin:** El Paso, Texas (1980s)
- **Operations:** Texas prisons and Mexican border areas.
- **Ideology:** Mexican-American loyalty; strong ties to Mexican drug cartels.
- **Activities:** Drug trafficking, murder, extortion, smuggling across the U.S.-Mexico border.
- **Identifying Features:**
    - Tattoos with Aztec symbols, "BA," or eagles and warriors.
    - Strong cartel affiliations, particularly with the Juárez Cartel.
    - Members communicate in Spanish and often use cartel slang.

10. Norteños

- **Origin:** Northern California, aligned with Nuestra Familia.
- **Operations:** Northern California and federal prisons.
- **Ideology:** Opposition to Sureños and Mexican Mafia.

- **Activities:** Drug distribution, extortion, and violent retaliation against Sureños.
- **Identifying Features:**
  - Tattoos with "14," "XIV," or "N."
  - Red clothing and bandanas.
  - Graffiti and symbols, often featuring Huelga birds or Aztec imagery.

Folk Nation

- **Origin:** Chicago, Illinois (1978)
- **Operations:** Nationwide, including prisons.
- **Ideology:** Loose alliance of gangs (e.g., Black Disciples, Gangster Disciples) unified under a set of rules.
- **Activities:** Drug trafficking, theft, and violence.
- **Identifying Features:**
  - Symbols: Six-pointed stars, pitchforks, hearts with wings.
  - Use of the number "6" in graffiti and tattoos.
  - Specific hand signs and phrases like "All is One."

People Nation

- **Origin:** Chicago, Illinois (1978)
- **Operations:** Nationwide, including prisons.
- **Ideology:** Counter to Folk Nation, with alliances among various gangs (e.g., Latin Kings, Vice Lords).
- **Activities:** Drug dealing, extortion, robbery.
- **Identifying Features:**
  - Symbols: Five-pointed stars, crowns, and pyramids.
  - Use of the number "5" in tattoos and graffiti.
  - Colors and symbols vary depending on the specific gang.

13. Texas Mexican Mafia (Mexikanemi)

- **Origin:** Texas Department of Criminal Justice (1984)
- **Operations:** Texas prisons and surrounding areas.

- **Ideology:** Mexican-American pride; separate from California's Mexican Mafia.
- **Activities:** Drug smuggling, murder-for-hire, extortion.
- **Identifying Features:**
  - Tattoos with "EME," "Mexikanemi," or images of Aztec warriors and eagles.
  - Use of Spanish language codes.
  - Members often align with specific cartels for drug distribution.

14. Hells Angels Motorcycle Club (Prison Affiliate)

- **Origin:** California (1948, with prison activities growing in the 1960s)
- **Operations:** Nationwide, including prisons.
- **Ideology:** Loyalty to the club and outlaw biker lifestyle.
- **Activities:** Drug manufacturing (especially meth), trafficking, and organized crime.
- **Identifying Features:**
  - Tattoos and patches with "H.A.," "81" (H = 8, A = 1), or winged skulls.
  - Red and white color scheme.
  - Strong loyalty to the motorcycle club hierarchy.

15. Sureños (South Siders)

- **Origin:** Southern California, with ties to the Mexican Mafia.
- **Operations:** Predominantly Southern California but found nationwide in federal and state prisons.
- **Ideology:** Loyalty to Mexican Mafia; rivalry with Norteños.
- **Activities:** Drug sales, extortion, violent assaults.
- **Identifying Features:**
  - Tattoos: "SUR," "13," "XIII."
  - Blue clothing and accessories.
  - Symbols like Aztec gods and imagery.

16. Nazi Low Riders (NLR)

- **Origin:** California Youth Authority (1970s)

- **Operations:** California, Nevada, Arizona, and Texas.
- **Ideology:** White supremacy, loyalty to the Aryan Brotherhood.
- **Activities:** Drug trafficking, assaults, extortion.
- **Identifying Features:**
    - Tattoos: "NLR," swastikas, lightning bolts, or eagles.
    - Wear white nationalist symbols and phrases.
    - Often act as enforcers for the Aryan Brotherhood.

17. Trinitarios

- **Origin:** New York City prisons (1990s)
- **Operations:** Northeastern U.S., particularly New York and New Jersey.
- **Ideology:** Dominican pride and unity.
- **Activities:** Drug trafficking, robberies, violent acts against rivals.
- **Identifying Features:**
    - Tattoos and graffiti with "D," "Trini," or "3NI."
    - Green clothing or accessories.
    - Use of machetes in violent confrontations.

18. Almighty Latin King and Queen Nation (Latin Kings)

- **Origin:** Chicago, Illinois (1940s)
- **Operations:** Nationwide, especially in the Midwest, New York, and Florida.
- **Ideology:** Latino unity and empowerment, heavily structured with a manifesto.
- **Activities:** Drug sales, murder, and robbery.
- **Identifying Features:**
    - Symbols: Five-pointed crowns, lions, or "LK" tattoos.
    - Black and gold clothing.
    - Known for highly organized meetings and codes of conduct.

19. The 415 Kumi Nation

- **Origin:** San Quentin State Prison, California (1980s)

- **Operations:** Northern California prisons and urban areas.
- **Ideology:** Black empowerment and resistance to other racial gangs.
- **Activities:** Drug sales, extortion, protection rackets.
- **Identifying Features:**
  - Tattoos: "415" (San Francisco area code), African symbols.
  - Members often adopt Afrocentric themes in tattoos and graffiti.

20. Dead Man Incorporated (DMI)

- **Origin:** Maryland prisons (2000s)
- **Operations:** Maryland and Mid-Atlantic states.
- **Ideology:** White inmates originally allied with the Black Guerrilla Family, later becoming independent.
- **Activities:** Drug trafficking, extortion, and violent enforcement.
- **Identifying Features:**
  - Tattoos: "DMI," Grim Reapers, or skulls.
  - Symbols of death and destruction.
  - Members maintain a violent reputation to gain respect.

21. Mandingo Warriors

- **Origin:** Texas prisons.
- **Operations:** Texas Department of Criminal Justice (TDCJ) facilities.
- **Ideology:** Black power and solidarity.
- **Activities:** Drug trafficking, extortion, protection rackets.
- **Identifying Features:**
  - Tattoos of African symbols, clenched fists, or the name "Mandingo."
  - Often aligned with other Black organizations within the prison system.

22. United Blood Nation (UBN)

- **Origin:** Rikers Island, New York (1993).
- **Operations:** East Coast prisons and urban areas.

- **Ideology:** Blood-affiliated street gang members united under a single umbrella.
- **Activities:** Drug sales, robberies, violent enforcement of gang rules.
- **Identifying Features:**
  - Tattoos: Five-pointed stars, "031" (code for "Blood Love"), or the letters "UBN."
  - Red clothing, bandanas, or accessories.

23. Vice Lords

- **Origin:** Chicago, Illinois (1950s).
- **Operations:** Midwest, Southeast, and East Coast prisons.
- **Ideology:** Black empowerment; part of the People Nation alliance.
- **Activities:** Drug trafficking, extortion, robberies.
- **Identifying Features:**
  - Symbols: Five-pointed stars, top hats, canes, and crescent moons.
  - Tattoos of initials "VL" or "Lord."
  - Use of gold and black as identifying colors.

24. Black Disciples

- **Origin:** Chicago, Illinois (1960s).
- **Operations:** Midwest and Northern states.
- **Ideology:** Black empowerment; affiliated with Folk Nation.
- **Activities:** Drug sales, murders, protection rackets.
- **Identifying Features:**
  - Symbols: Six-pointed stars, pitchforks, or devil horns.
  - Tattoos of initials "BD."
  - Blue or black clothing.

25. 18th Street Gang

- **Origin:** Los Angeles, California (1960s).
- **Operations:** Nationwide, especially in the Southwest and federal prisons.

- **Ideology:** Latino pride and extreme loyalty to the gang.
- **Activities:** Drug trafficking, violent crimes, human smuggling.
- **Identifying Features:**
    - Tattoos with "18," "XVIII," or "666" (sum of 18).
    - Blue and black colors.
    - Graffiti with the number 18 or variations.

26. Tiny Rascal Gang (TRG)

- **Origin:** Long Beach, California (1980s).
- **Operations:** West Coast, especially California and Washington.
- **Ideology:** Southeast Asian pride, predominantly Cambodian-American.
- **Activities:** Drug trafficking, violent crimes, robbery.
- **Identifying Features:**
    - Tattoos with "TRG" or "712" (TRG = 20th, 18th, and 7th letters of the alphabet).
    - Use of gray clothing or accessories.
    - Strong loyalty to gang elders.

27. Hermanos de Pistoleros Latinos (HPL)

- **Origin:** Texas prisons (1980s).
- **Operations:** Texas and surrounding border states.
- **Ideology:** Latino solidarity and cartel alliances.
- **Activities:** Drug smuggling, extortion, murder-for-hire.
- **Identifying Features:**
    - Tattoos with "HPL," pistols, or imagery of Texas/Mexico.
    - Spanish language codes and graffiti.

28. Sureños Cliques (Southside Affiliates)

- **Origin:** Southern California (aligned with the Mexican Mafia).
- **Operations:** State prisons and urban areas nationwide.
- **Ideology:** Loyalty to La Eme; rivalry with Norteños.
- **Activities:** Drug trafficking, violent enforcement, territory control.

- **Identifying Features:**
  - Numbers like "13," "XIII," or "Sur."
  - Tattoos with Aztec themes or blue color schemes.

29. Peckerwoods

- **Origin:** California prisons (1960s).
- **Operations:** West Coast and Texas prisons.
- **Ideology:** White supremacist ideology, lower-level allies of the Aryan Brotherhood.
- **Activities:** Drug trafficking, extortion, violence.
- **Identifying Features:**
  - Tattoos of woodpeckers, swastikas, or lightning bolts.
  - Symbols of Nordic mythology or white supremacy.

30. Ghost Shadows

- **Origin:** New York City Chinatown (1970s).
- **Operations:** East Coast and federal prisons.
- **Ideology:** Chinese-American gang focused on protection and financial power.
- **Activities:** Extortion, gambling rings, drug sales.
- **Identifying Features:**
  - Tattoos with dragons or Chinese characters.
  - Subtle identification, as gang members often try to blend in.

31. Zetas Prison Affiliates

- **Origin:** Mexican military deserters forming the Zetas cartel in the 1990s.
- **Operations:** U.S.-Mexico border prisons.
- **Ideology:** Cartel loyalty and extreme violence.
- **Activities:** Drug and human trafficking, murders, extortion.
- **Identifying Features:**
  - Tattoos with Zetas symbols, Mexican military imagery.

    ○ High levels of violence and military tactics.

32. Mexican Posse

- **Origin:** Arizona Department of Corrections (1990s).
- **Operations:** Arizona and nearby states.
- **Ideology:** Loyalty to Latino culture and organized crime.
- **Activities:** Drug trafficking, assaults.
- **Identifying Features:**
  - Tattoos with "MP" or variations.
  - Southwest cultural imagery.

33. Nuestra Raza

- **Origin:** Splinter group of Nuestra Familia.
- **Operations:** Northern California prisons.
- **Ideology:** Subset focused on secrecy and control within the Norteños.
- **Activities:** Internal governance, violent enforcement, drug trafficking.
- **Identifying Features:**
  - Tattoos with "NR" or Huelga bird imagery.
  - Tight affiliation with Norteños' color schemes and codes.

34. Tangos (Texas Area Gangs Organization)

- **Origin:** Texas prisons (1990s).
- **Operations:** Texas and federal prisons.
- **Ideology:** Regional loyalty based on Texas cities (Houston, Austin, Dallas, etc.).
- **Activities:** Protection rackets, drug trafficking, and violence.
- **Identifying Features:**
  - Tattoos with city abbreviations (e.g., "H" for Houston, "D" for Dallas).
  - Regional slang and specific symbols.

35. White Knights

- **Origin:** Southern U.S. prisons.

- **Operations:** Southeastern states, particularly Mississippi and Alabama.
- **Ideology:** White supremacy and KKK-affiliated beliefs.
- **Activities:** Hate crimes, drug distribution.
- **Identifying Features:**
  - Tattoos with Confederate flags, swastikas, or KKK symbols.
  - Graffiti referencing white nationalist themes.

36. Black Mafia Family (BMF)

- **Origin:** Detroit, Michigan (1980s).
- **Operations:** Nationwide, especially in Midwest and Southern prisons.
- **Ideology:** African-American organized crime syndicate.
- **Activities:** Large-scale drug distribution, financial crimes.
- **Identifying Features:**
  - Tattoos with "BMF" or crowns.
  - Subtle markings, as the organization operates with discipline.

37. Crips

- **Origin:** Los Angeles, California (1960s)
- **Operations:** Nationwide, especially in urban areas and prisons across the U.S.
- **Ideology:** Initially focused on community protection, now known for organized crime and territorial control.
- **Activities:** Drug trafficking, assaults, extortion, and rivalries with Bloods.
- **Identifying Features:**
  - Tattoos with "C," "BK" (Blood Killer), or six-pointed stars.
  - Blue clothing, bandanas, and accessories.
  - Graffiti often includes the number "6" or references to Folk Nation.

38. Bloods

- **Origin:** Los Angeles, California (1970s)
- **Operations:** Nationwide, with a strong presence in East Coast prisons and urban centers.

- **Ideology:** Formed as a response to Crips' dominance; focused on unity and control of territory.
- **Activities:** Drug distribution, violence, extortion, and rivalry with Crips.
- **Identifying Features:**
  - Tattoos with "B," "CK" (Crip Killer), or five-pointed stars.
  - Red clothing, bandanas, and accessories.
  - Graffiti with the number "5" or references to People Nation.

CON GAMES MODULE NINE

How to Check an Inmate & Report Harassment

Ladies, listen up. If you're in a relationship with a man on the inside—or even just entertaining letters—you can't afford to fly blind. You need receipts. You need to know exactly where he is, what he's locked up for, and how to shut him down if he crosses the line. This ain't about being nosy—it's about survival.

Step 1: Verify His Status — Don't Take His Word for It

These men will spin fairy tales about why they're inside. Some will soften the charges ("just a misunderstanding"), others will straight-up invent stories ("they framed me"). Here's how you cut through the bullshit:

1. **Federal Prisoners (BOP):**

   - Go to the **Federal Bureau of Prisons Inmate Locator** (bop.gov/inmateloc).
   - Type his name or register number.
   - If he's in federal custody, it'll show you his facility, release date, and number.

2. **State Prisoners (DOC):**

   - Every state has its own **Department of Corrections website** with an inmate search tool.

   - Plug in his full name and DOB. If he's in state custody, you'll find him.

3. **County Jail / Local Lockup:**

   ○ Check the **county sheriff's website**. Many post daily booking logs and rosters.
   ○ If he's fresh in or waiting on trial, this is where he'll pop up.

4. **VINELink (National):**

   ○ VINELink.com is a victim notification network. You can track inmate location and even sign up for alerts on transfers or release dates.

5. **If You're Still Stuck:**

   ○ Call the **court clerk** where his case was handled. Ask for custody status.
   ○ Or call the **county jail intake** directly and give them his name + DOB.

Red Flag Check: If he tells you he's in the feds but his name doesn't show up in the BOP system? He's lying. Already.

Step 2: Get the Paperwork — Charges Don't Lie

Words are cheap. Paper isn't. Here's where you find the truth:

- **Court Records:**

  ○ Most counties have online dockets you can search by name. You'll see his case number, charges, sentencing, and hearing dates.

- **PACER (Federal Cases):**

  ○ Federal charges live in PACER (Public Access to Court Electronic Records). There's a small fee, but it's worth it.

- **Ask for the PSI/PSR (Pre-Sentence Report):**

  - If you're deep with him, this document is gold. It lays out everything he did, how much loss was calculated, and how the sentence was decided. If he refuses to show you? He's hiding something.

Step 3: When Harassment Starts — Lock It Down

Now let's get to the ugly part. If he crosses the line—threats, extortion, nonstop calls, manipulative letters—you need to move fast and smart.

1. **Stop engaging.**

   - Every reply gives him fuel. Silence is your first weapon.

2. **Document EVERYTHING.**

   - Save every letter.
   - Take photos of envelopes with postmarks.
   - Screenshot texts, emails, social media messages.
   - Keep call logs and voicemails.
   - Save JPay receipts or money transfer records.
   - Write down dates, times, and details in a simple notebook.

3. **Report to the Facility.**

   - Call the warden's office or shift commander: "I'm a civilian being harassed by inmate [name/inmate number]. I want it logged."

   - Send a written complaint to the Warden (use certified mail if you can). Attach copies of evidence. Keep copies for yourself.

4. **Go Through Victim Channels.**

   - **PREA Coordinator:** Every prison has one. Report sexual harassment or abuse. They're required to investigate.

o **Victim Services Office:** Ask the DOC/BOP to register you as a victim so you get updates and protections.

5. **Local Police.**

   o If there are threats, extortion, or stalking, file a police report. That creates a case number that forces the prison to take you seriously.

6. **Financial Protection.**
   o If he got money out of you, contact the vendor (JPay, Western Union, MoneyGram) for transaction records.

   o Report fraud to your bank and block future transfers.

7. **Legal & Protective Orders.**

   o Harassment from prison can be the basis for a restraining order. Talk to an attorney or victim advocate about filing.

Step 4: Escalate if They Stall

Prisons drag their feet. Don't let that stall you. If nothing happens after you report:

- **For Federal Inmates:**

   o File an **Administrative Remedy (BP-9)**. If ignored, escalate to BP-10 (regional) and BP-11 (national).

- **For State Inmates:**

   o Escalate to the **central DOC office** or the **state attorney general's office**.

- **For Both:**

   o Contact your local victim advocacy groups (domestic violence shelters, legal aid). They know how to push the system.

Sample Letter to Report Inmate Harassment

[Your Full Name]
[Your Address]
[City, State, ZIP]
[Phone Number]
[Email Address]
[Date]

Warden [Warden's Full Name]
[Facility Name]
[Facility Address]
[City, State, ZIP]

Subject: Formal Complaint – Harassment by Inmate [Inmate Full Name / Inmate Number]

Dear Warden [Last Name],

My name is [Your Full Name], and I am writing to formally report repeated harassment by inmate [Inmate Full Name], inmate number [#], currently housed at [Facility Name]. I request immediate action to stop all unwanted communication and to protect me from further harassment.

Summary of Harassment:

- On [date], I received [letter/call/message] that contained [describe briefly: threats, sexual harassment, manipulation, extortion, etc.].

- On [date], I received [second incident].
- This behavior has caused me [fear, emotional distress, financial loss, safety concerns].

Evidence Provided:

- Copies of letters, envelopes, and emails.
- Screenshots of text messages or social media.
- Call logs/voicemails.
- Proof of money requests or transactions ([JPay, Western Union, MoneyGram, etc.]).

Requested Actions:

1. Place inmate [Full Name] on **no-contact status** with me, effective immediately.
2. Monitor and block future calls, letters, emails, or messages from this inmate.
3. Investigate the harassment in compliance with PREA (Prison Rape Elimination Act) and institutional policies.
4. Provide me with written confirmation of actions taken within [14] days.

For additional documentation, I have also filed a report with [local police department / other authority], case/report number [#], on [date].

I am requesting this matter be taken seriously and handled promptly. Please confirm receipt of this complaint and advise me of next steps.

Sincerely,
[Your Signature]
[Your Printed Name]

Attachments:
[List everything included: copies of letters, screenshots, receipts, police report, etc.]

Sample Letter – Inmate Harassment Complaint

Jane Smith
123 Main Street
Atlanta, GA 30303
(555) 555-1212
janesmith@email.com
March 5, 2025

Warden Robert Jackson
Smith State Prison
123 Prison Road
Savannah, GA 31401

Subject: Formal Complaint – Harassment by Inmate Devon Williams #445667

Dear Warden Jackson,

My name is Jane Smith, and I am writing to file a formal complaint regarding harassment by inmate **Devon Williams**, inmate number **445667**, currently housed at **Smith State Prison**.

Over the past two months, I have received multiple unwanted letters and phone calls from Mr. Williams, despite making it clear that I do not wish to have any contact with him. These communications have included repeated requests for money, manipulative statements designed to guilt me, and most recently, threatening language that has caused me significant distress.

Summary of Harassment:

- **January 15, 2025** – I received a letter asking me to send $200 through JPay and implying that "bad things would happen" if I did not.

- **February 2, 2025** – I received two phone calls where the inmate used verbally abusive language after I refused to accept his requests.

- **February 18, 2025** – Another letter was delivered, this time threatening to contact my family members if I did not send funds.

Evidence Provided:

- Copies of the original letters and envelopes (attached).
- JPay transfer request screenshots.
- Phone logs showing calls from the facility.

Requested Actions:

1. Immediately place inmate **Devon Williams #445667** on **no-contact status** with me.
2. Monitor and block all future communications (mail, phone, electronic) from this inmate.
3. Investigate this matter in accordance with facility policy and PREA standards.
4. Provide written confirmation within 14 days regarding what actions have been taken.

For your records, I have also filed a report with the **Atlanta Police Department** (case number 2025-APD-11984, filed on February 20, 2025).

This situation has caused me both financial loss and emotional harm, and I am requesting swift action to ensure it does not continue. Please confirm receipt of this complaint and advise me of the steps being taken.

Sincerely,
 Jane Smith

Attachments:

- Letter dated January 15, 2025
- Letter dated February 18, 2025
- JPay request screenshot
- Phone log records

Quick Complaint Letter – Inmate Harassment

[Your Name]
[Your Address]
[City, State, ZIP]
[Phone Number]
[Email Address]
[Date]

Warden [Warden's Full Name]
[Facility Name]
[Facility Address]
[City, State, ZIP]

Subject: Urgent Complaint – Harassment by Inmate [Inmate Name / Inmate Number]

Dear Warden [Last Name],

I am writing to formally report **harassment by inmate [Inmate Full Name / Inmate Number]** currently housed at your facility.

I have received **unwanted communication** in the form of [letters / phone calls / emails] that include [briefly state: threats, requests for money, manipulative or abusive language]. I do not wish to have any further contact with this inmate.

Requested Actions:

- Immediately block all communication from inmate [Full Name].
- Investigate the matter according to facility policy and PREA standards.
- Provide written confirmation of what actions are being taken.

This harassment has caused me serious distress, and I am requesting immediate action to protect my safety and peace of mind.

Sincerely,
[Your Signature]
[Your Printed Name]

Keisha's Bottom Line

These men will play on your kindness, your guilt, and your loyalty. Knowing where they are and what they're really in for strips away their power to lie. Reporting their harassment strips away their power to control you.

So don't sit there hoping he'll "change." Don't tell yourself it's "just letters." Once it starts, it doesn't stop until **you** stop it.

Stay sharp. Stay in control. And never forget—you don't owe an inmate your silence, your peace, or your damn wallet.

—**Keisha**

<u>Sample Letter to Report Inmate Harassment</u>

[Your Full Name]
[Your Address]
[City, State, ZIP]
[Phone Number]
[Email Address]
[Date]

Warden [Warden's Full Name]
[Facility Name]
[Facility Address]
[City, State, ZIP]

Subject: Formal Complaint – Harassment by Inmate [Inmate Full Name / Inmate Number]

Dear Warden [Last Name],

My name is [Your Full Name], and I am writing to formally report repeated harassment by inmate [Inmate Full Name], inmate number [#], currently housed at [Facility Name]. I request immediate action to stop all unwanted communication and to protect me from further harassment.

Summary of Harassment:

- On [date], I received [letter/call/message] that contained [describe briefly: threats, sexual harassment, manipulation, extortion, etc.].
- On [date], I received [second incident].
- This behavior has caused me [fear, emotional distress, financial loss, safety concerns].

Evidence Provided:

- Copies of letters, envelopes, and emails.
- Screenshots of text messages or social media.
- Call logs/voicemails.
- Proof of money requests or transactions ([JPay, Western Union, MoneyGram, etc.]).

Requested Actions:

1. Place inmate [Full Name] on **no-contact status** with me, effective immediately.
2. Monitor and block future calls, letters, emails, or messages from this inmate.
3. Investigate the harassment in compliance with PREA (Prison Rape Elimination Act) and institutional policies.
4. Provide me with written confirmation of actions taken within [14] days.

For additional documentation, I have also filed a report with [local police department / other authority], case/report number [#], on [date].

I am requesting this matter be taken seriously and handled promptly. Please confirm receipt of this complaint and advise me of next steps.

Sincerely,
[Your Signature]
[Your Printed Name]

Attachments:
[List everything included: copies of letters, screenshots, receipts, police report, etc.]

Sample Letter – Inmate Harassment Complaint

Jane Smith
123 Main Street
Atlanta, GA 30303
(555) 555-1212
janesmith@email.com
March 5, 2025

Warden Robert Jackson
Smith State Prison
123 Prison Road
Savannah, GA 31401

Subject: Formal Complaint – Harassment by Inmate Devon Williams #445667

Dear Warden Jackson,

My name is Jane Smith, and I am writing to file a formal complaint regarding harassment by inmate **Devon Williams**, inmate number **445667**, currently housed at **Smith State Prison**.

Over the past two months, I have received multiple unwanted letters and phone calls from Mr. Williams, despite making it clear that I do not wish to have any contact with him. These communications have included repeated requests for money, manipulative statements designed to guilt me, and most recently, threatening language that has caused me significant distress.

Summary of Harassment:

- **January 15, 2025** – I received a letter asking me to send $200 through JPay and implying that "bad things would happen" if I did not.

- **February 2, 2025** – I received two phone calls where the inmate used verbally abusive language after I refused to accept his requests.

- **February 18, 2025** – Another letter was delivered, this time threatening to contact my family members if I did not send funds.

Evidence Provided:

- Copies of the original letters and envelopes (attached).
- JPay transfer request screenshots.
- Phone logs showing calls from the facility.

Requested Actions:

1. Immediately place inmate **Devon Williams #445667** on **no-contact status** with me.
2. Monitor and block all future communications (mail, phone, electronic) from this inmate.
3. Investigate this matter in accordance with facility policy and PREA standards.
4. Provide written confirmation within 14 days regarding what actions have been taken.

For your records, I have also filed a report with the **Atlanta Police Department** (case number 2025-APD-11984, filed on February 20, 2025).

This situation has caused me both financial loss and emotional harm, and I am requesting swift action to ensure it does not continue. Please confirm receipt of this complaint and advise me of the steps being taken.

Sincerely,
Jane Smith

Attachments:

- Letter dated January 15, 2025
- Letter dated February 18, 2025
- JPay request screenshot
- Phone log records

Quick Complaint Letter – Inmate Harassment

[Your Name]
[Your Address]
[City, State, ZIP]
[Phone Number]
[Email Address]
[Date]

Warden [Warden's Full Name]
[Facility Name]
[Facility Address]
[City, State, ZIP]

Subject: Urgent Complaint – Harassment by Inmate [Inmate Name / Inmate Number]

Dear Warden [Last Name],

I am writing to formally report **harassment by inmate [Inmate Full Name / Inmate Number]** currently housed at your facility.

I have received **unwanted communication** in the form of [letters / phone calls / emails] that include [briefly state: threats, requests for money, manipulative or abusive language]. I do not wish to have any further contact with this inmate.

Requested Actions:

- Immediately block all communication from inmate [Full Name].
- Investigate the matter according to facility policy and PREA standards.
- Provide written confirmation of what actions are being taken.

This harassment has caused me serious distress, and I am requesting immediate action to protect my safety and peace of mind.

Sincerely,
[Your Signature]
[Your Printed Name]

EPILOUGE

CON GAMES & LOVE SCAMS

Ladies — let me lay it down plain. If you've read every page of this book, that means something deep inside you already knew. You knew the letters didn't add up. You knew the phone calls felt a little too scripted. You knew that every "baby, I love you" came with a shadow of "now what you gonna do for me?"

I didn't write this just to point fingers at inmates. I wrote this for you — the women who give, the women who love, the women who believe. Because I've been you. I know what it's like to wait on a phone call like it's oxygen. I know what it's like to reread a letter until the ink feels tattooed on your heart. I know what it's like to defend a man to everyone around you, only to find out later he was running the same game on two or three other women. That kind of betrayal don't just hurt your feelings — it shakes your whole damn identity.

But let me say this loud: **you are not weak because you cared.** You are not dumb because you trusted. You are not pathetic because you wanted to believe in love, even when it came wrapped in barbed wire. That just makes you human. What makes you stronger is sitting here now, facing the truth, and saying: *"Not again. Not me. Not this time."*

I want you to carry that strength with you long after you close this book. Don't just think of these chapters as stories — think of them as survival maps. Every letter I tore apart, every hustle I exposed, every scam I broke down — those are red flags you now know how to spot before they cost you your money, your sanity, and your damn self-worth. Use them. Share them. Hand this book to another woman who needs it. Make it the wall between you and the next con artist with a DOC number.

Now let me get personal. This book didn't just come out of my mouth. It came out of real scars — mine and Larry Levine's. Larry lived this system from the inside. He saw the games up close in the cellblocks and the yards. I lived the other side — the women who got caught in the crossfire. Together, we brought both sides of the hustle into one place, so no one can say they didn't know anymore. This is the warning label the system will never give you.

Larry and I didn't do this to shame anyone. We did it to protect you. We did it so you don't have to learn the hardest lessons the hardest way. We did it so maybe the next time some man calls you "queen" from behind a prison wall, you'll pause, breathe, and ask yourself: *"Is this real, or is this game?"* And then you'll have the power to walk away if it's the latter.

So yeah, this is sappy. It's personal. It's me pouring my guts out. But it's also the truth: **you deserve better than being somebody's hustle.** You deserve love that don't come with a commissary bill. You deserve loyalty that ain't written on ruled notebook paper with a hidden price tag in the third paragraph. You deserve peace, joy, and respect that doesn't vanish the second you say "no" to sending money.

Promise yourself right now: you'll never trade your dignity for a few sweet words again.

And when you hear from one of these smooth-talking jailhouse poets trying to play the same old violin, I hope you hear my voice cutting through the noise, saying: *"Girl, don't fall for that shit again."*

From my heart to yours — I love y'all enough to tell you the truth, even when it stings. And Larry Levine? He stood beside me on this project to make sure it cut as sharp as it needed to. His years in the belly of the beast, my years on the outside learning the hard way — put together, that's the shield you're holding now. Use it. Protect yourself. Share it with the women who need it.

Because at the end of the day? You ain't just surviving. You're rising.

— **Keisha**

www.ingramcontent.com/pod-product-compliance
Lightning Source LLC
Chambersburg PA
CBHW080402270326
41927CB00015B/3323